GREENSAND

WAY

IN KENT

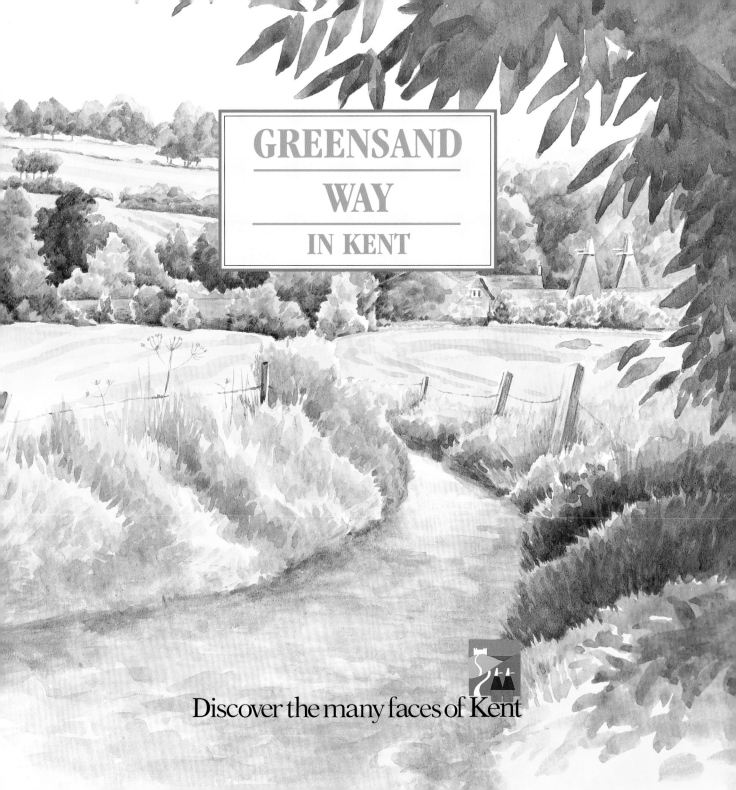

GREENSAND
WAY
IN KENT

Discover the many faces of Kent

Designed and produced by
Countryside Group and County Visuals,
Kent County Council,
Planning Department.

Narrative text by Bea Cowan.
Watercolour illustrations by Sandra Fernandez.
Photographs by Brian Owen.

Maps produced by County Visuals
with the sanction of the Controller of
HM Stationery Office.
Crown Copyright reserved.

Printed in Great Britain by
Springfield Litho,
Sevenoaks, Kent.

Published by Kent County Council,
Planning Department,
Springfield, Maidstone, Kent
ME14 2LX.

First published June 1992.

ISBN 1 873010 23 0

CONTENTS

To the best of our knowledge the historical content and all other information is believed to be correct. We would be grateful if you would inform us of any changes, omissions or errors, so that modifications can be made in subsequent revisions of the book.

INTRODUCTION

The Greensand Way is a long distance walking route extending for some 100 miles across Surrey and Kent. Its origins go back to the 1970s when Geoffrey Hollis, a well-known member of the Ramblers' Association in Surrey at that time, proposed the route. It was supported by the then Surrey Amenity Council and the Surrey Voluntary Services Council, and the first section was opened crossing Leith Hill to celebrate Footpath Heritage Year in 1980.

The route has since been developed by the Surrey County Council which, like the Kent County Council, sees the Greensand Way as an important amenity that contributes to the increasing public demand for access to the countryside. A guide to the whole of the Surrey section that begins in Haslemere and ends at the county boundary near Limpsfield Chart, is published by the Surrey County Council (see below).

The Ramblers' Association in Kent began planning the extension to the Greensand Way in the early 1980s, and the first 22½ mile West Kent section from the Surrey border to Yalding was opened on 13 April 1986. Supported by Kent County Council, a route guide was published consisting of a pack of walk cards. The 32½ mile East Kent section was planned by the Maidstone and Ashford Groups of the Ramblers' Association, and the whole route was formally opened in April 1989 by Fay Godwin, who was then President of the Ramblers' Association. It was supported by a walk cards pack published in collaboration with Kent County Council.

Within the Council's Countryside and Rights of Way Strategies approved in 1989, was an undertaking to develop recreational walking routes in response

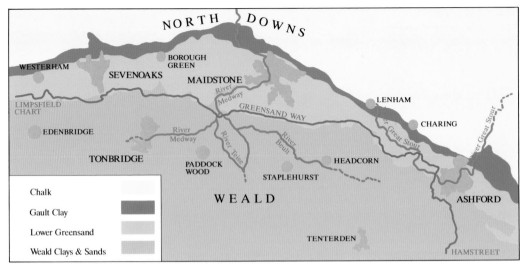

to the evident demand by the public for better access to the countryside. Having successfully developed the Stour Valley and Eden Valley Walks, Kent County Council in 1991 offered to improve the Greensand Way and publish a matching guide. The earlier RA guides were, by this time, in need of updating, since many features in the landscape had been changed, not least by the hurricane of October 1987 which destroyed vast areas

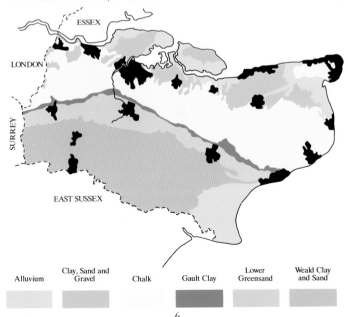

of woodland along the Greensand ridge. This new guide is the result of a close collaboration between Kent County Council and the Ramblers' Association. It is hoped that all who walk this section of the Greensand Way will enjoy some of the finest countryside in Kent.

Copies of the guide to the Surrey section of the Greensand Way (price £2.50) may be obtained from: Public Relations Unit,

County Hall, Kingston upon Thames, Surrey KT1 2DN.

GREENSAND RIDGE

Geology

The name 'Greensand' comes from the green coloured mineral glauconite which is unevenly distributed throughout the rock and, when present in significant amounts, gives it a greenish tinge. On exposure to the atmosphere, it is oxidised giving rise to yellow staining.

Around 140 million years ago, the rocks now found in the central Weald were first deposited in shallow brackish water. Twenty million years later the sea broke into this Wealden lake and the rock of the Lower Greensand formation were deposited over a period of about ten million years.

The Hythe Beds, consisting of a calcareous sandstone or ragstone, form the escarpment itself, the highest range of hills along which the majority of the Greensand Way runs. From the Surrey border in the west to Pluckley in the east, the escarpment of the Lower Greensand Hythe Beds is a marked feature increasing in height westwards to a maximum of 245 metres at Toys Hill.

At the end of this ten million years, in which Lower Greensand deposits were laid down, the sea gradually deepened and first Gault Clay, then the Upper Greensand, followed by a thick deposit of chalk of which the North Downs are composed, were laid down.

There followed a gradual uplifting and folding of the rocks. Erosion by wind and water partially removed the younger rocks from this Wealden dome to form the chalk and sandstone hills, and expose the Wealden sands and clays. Since then, continual erosion has gradually carved out the present features of the landscape.

All the sandstones have been extensively quarried over the centuries for building, road materials and sand. The stone gives rise to the characteristic ragstone buildings which can be seen along the Way.

Natural History

The ridges associated with the Lower Greensand extend from Folkestone in the east to Hampshire in the west. In many places these ridges stand out quite spectacularly from the clay vales, to help create the ridge and vale landscape that typifies large areas of the Weald.

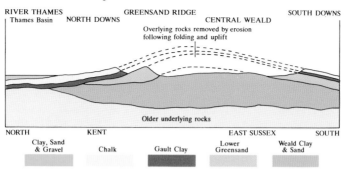

Outline Geological Section across the Downs and Weald

RIVER THAMES — Thames Basin — NORTH DOWNS — GREENSAND RIDGE — CENTRAL WEALD — SOUTH DOWNS

Overlying rocks removed by erosion following folding and uplift

Older underlying rocks

NORTH — KENT — EAST SUSSEX — SOUTH

Clay, Sand & Gravel | Chalk | Gault Clay | Lower Greensand | Weald Clay & Sand

The Lower Greensand is made up of a series of quite distinct formations and the natural vegetation associated with it varies according to the soil type present. This in turn varies with the properties of the parent material. In the case of the greensand, the beds vary from sand and clay to sandy limestone. Soils vary from the more acidic to calcareous where they are derived from the ragstone.

In very general terms the soils found on the Greensand ridge in Kent tend to be richer than those over the border to the west, where large tracts of heathland occur. However, a few outcrops of heathland can be seen along the route, most notably that at Hothfield Common near Ashford. Here the sandy soils, derived from the Folkestone Beds within the Greensand series, give rise to a vegetation dominated by heather, bracken and birch. Small acid peat mires occur which support some locally unusual plant species including the insectivorous sundew. The Common itself has been designated a Site of Special Scientific Interest and is managed as a nature reserve by the Kent Trust for Nature Conservation.

The Kentish ragstone that forms part of the series breaks down in places to give fertile and well drained loam soils. This gives rise to good quality arable farmland, particularly towards the eastern end of the outcrop. Where the natural vegetation remains on these loam soils, woodland dominates, with good stands of oak and with a hazel understorey.

From close to Ashford westward, the Greensand escarpment increases in height towards Toys Hill near Westerham and is even higher across the border into Surrey.

Much of the woodland of the Greensand ridge was devastated during the great storm of October 1987. At Toys Hill, the landscape is almost unrecognisable from previous years. As a result of the storm, the former mature oak and beech-covered hill is now virtually devoid of any mature trees. Instead, much of the woodland floor is covered with young silver birch, a natural coloniser of greensand.

A walk along the Greensand Way will reveal the tremendous diversity of habitats along this outcrop. At Crockhamhill Common the path passes through woodland, particularly in those areas sheltered from the 1987 storm. Here the path follows narrow eroded channels in the sandy floor surrounded by good stands of silver birch and some Scots pine - a natural tree of Greensand. Oak and sweet chestnut are also present. Bilberry and bracken occur here and in several other places along the route. Both flourish in the more acid soils. Birds likely to be seen here include blue tit, coal tit, great tit, goldcrest and chaffinch.

From Toys Hill to the east of Ide Hill, much of the route passes through a Site of Special Scientific Interest (SSSI). The site has been designated an SSSI largely because of the rich woodland habitat. The woodland is dominated by birch, beech and oak, including the best stands of sessile oak in Kent. Birch is particularly prevalent along this section of the route.

Here, areas now open as a result of the 1987 storm have been colonised by plants such as broom and rosebay willowherb. Butterflies are plentiful in these clearings and include red admiral, meadow brown and gatekeeper.

At Knole Park the natural vegetation is replaced with a parkland habitat. Here there are many fine specimen trees including oak, beech and sweet chestnut. The bracken provides cover for the large number of deer resident in the park. A wide variety of bird species have been recorded here including green and great spotted woodpecker, treecreeper and nuthatch.

Fallow Deer

Hanging baskets at Yalding

At Ightham Mote the use of greensand as a local building stone is evident. It is interesting to study the variations in the Greensand series by looking at the 'geology of the buildings' along the route.

From Sutton Valence eastwards the Greensand ridge becomes steadily lower and the scenery changes to one dominated by farmland with scattered hedgerows and small stands of trees. This provides an interesting contrast with the steeper and higher land to the west.

Archaeology and History

Kent's archaeological history began over a quarter of a million years ago and rich remains relating to all periods have been found across the County. The various regions of Kent are characterised by differing geologies and landscapes and as a consequence the particular areas developed at varying speeds and in different ways. The Greensand Way follows the southern edge of the rocky Greensand ridge which overlooks the Weald. Historically this area is known as the 'Chartland' a term which reflects its geological provenance. 'Chart' is a word of Norwegian origin meaning 'rough, rocky, sterile ground', and it is an element found in many place names on the stone hills. Although the narrow winding valleys that cut through this

Stone carving at Boughton Malherbe Church

stony area are comparatively sheltered, green and well watered, the occupation of the 'Chartland' seems to stem mainly from the medieval period. There are, however, exceptions and remains dating from earlier times have survived.

Glimpses into early prehistory have been provided in Ightham Parish and around Dunk's Green where many Palaeolithic and Neolithic artefacts have been found. Bronze Age pottery and artefacts are known in this same area and an isolated barrow or burial mound site lies on the slopes above Egerton. Centuries later several of the stone hills were occupied when Iron Age communities constructed massive earthwork ramparts at Squerryes Park Camp (Westerham), Oldbury Hill (Ightham), and Boughton Camp (Boughton Monchelsea). The possible outworks of the Boughton Camp lies just 100 metres north of the Greensand Way. Sites such as Boughton Camp, classically referred to as 'oppida' are the topic of continued debate and while few have been the subject of a modern excavation these places may have been incipient towns.

Although much of this region was generally inaccessible, the Romans established communication and trade routes across the landscape. Their road alignments from Maidstone through to Hastings and also to Lympne Fort are crossed by the Greensand Way. Little is visible but these routes divided just west of Chart Sutton, with the Hastings road taking a long straight route across the Low Weald towards Staplehurst and the Maidstone to Lympne alignment heading south-east through to Sutton Valence. This second road is seen again south of Ashford in the parishes of Great Chart and Kingsnorth.

Remains including pottery, coins, building debris and a substantial cemetery provide evidence for a Roman

Detail of Bell House at Boughton Malherbe

settlement in the Sutton Valence area. Small farmsteads grew up in other parts of the 'Chartland'. The most well known are the villas at Plaxtol one of which has recently been investigated by the Kent Archaeological Society. Stone quarries at One Tree Hill near Sevenoaks and South Beers Wood have revealed small burial groups.

During the Medieval period the essential character of the Greensand area was established. By the tenth or eleventh century the ridge was reasonably well settled and churches and parishes became established across much of the 'Chartland'. The fortified Norman castle at Sutton Valence symbolises the feudal system that was developing. Excavations carried out by the local school suggest that this keep was in use between the mid twelfth and late thirteenth century. Twelve medieval churches lie close to the Greensand Way and most hold prominent positions in the landscape. Each is fascinating but a particular highlight is the wall painting at All Saints Church in Ulcombe.

In the following centuries many new manors were established. These included famous seats such as Knole, Squerryes, and the beautifully preserved Ightham Mote. Most of the distinguished manors originating

between 1250 and 1350 were surrounded by a moat. Many are known in Kent and others close to the footpath include the remains at Fairlawne in Shipbourne, and those at Court Lodge Farm and Park Farm in Kingsnorth.

The prosperity of these manors varied considerably, some apparently on a constantly upward spiral with others declining after just a century of occupation. The palatial buildings and extensive parkland at Knole reflect the estate's associations with the Archbishops of Canterbury, with Henry VIII and with the aristocratic Sackvilles. The Greensand Way passes along the southern edge of the parkland (originally a deer park). Of additional interest are the medieval and post-medieval glassworks located just west of Knole Park. According to the Knole accounts these works were fired with fuel from the estate. Other smaller estates developed their parklands, initially for deer but then for ornament. The grounds of Boughton Place which lie immediately south of the Greensand Way are a good example. The parkland at Godinton, north-west of Ashford, was originally established in Norman times but the present house is of seventeenth century date and many elements of this landscape are attributable to the seventeenth, nineteenth and twentieth centuries.

Communications were improved during the period. Two skilfully constructed ragstone bridges, one in Yalding Town which spans the River Beult and adjoining marshes and a second, the Twyford Bridge which is distinctive for its four irregular pointed arches, are testimony to this. Work resulting from the Medway Navigation Act in 1740 enhanced the commerical potential of the river. A fine example of this is the Hampstead Canal which cut across a broad loop of the river at Yalding.

From the top of the escarpment near Hamstreet there is a panoramic view of Romney Marsh. Most of the visible elements in the landscape have evolved in the last two centuries but many important archaeological sites lie on or just below the surface of the marsh. That is, of course, a different story.

GREENSAND WAY LOGO

The design of the Greensand Way logo is based on the oast-house which, with its distinctive cowl, is a traditional feature of the Kent countryside.

These buildings were used to dry hops in readiness for beer- making. The word oast is so named from the old English word for drying. In the early days of hop growing, the fruit, known as the 'cone', was dried in the sun. This method was clearly unreliable and farmers started to dry their hops in standard barns. Then, once the hop industry had become established and the outlay was considered worth-while, farmers developed a system of drying indoors.

The design of the oast-house, originally rectangular, and looking much like the standard barn, was introduced from Holland in the seventeenth century. The building contained three rooms, one for loading, one for drying, one for cooling.

Square oast houses followed, then, in the early nineteenth century, round, as drying techniques changed. Finally the square form returned to favour. The cowl, traditionally made by a wheelwright, evolved at the end of the eighteenth century. It formed a crucial part of the structure, being designed to

create a vacuum which would draw the hot air through the oast-house. The characteristic wind vane, extending from the cowl, was a nineteenth century addition.

The position of the vane varies from oast to oast. In mid Kent you will find it near the base of the cowl. In east Kent, where the vane is far shorter, you will find it at the top. The vane was frequently embellished with a finial, often with a motif, the favourite motif in Kent being the horse rampant.

Hop Growing

Hops were first introduced into Kent from Flanders at the end of the fifteenth century. At first many people opposed the use of hops in beer considering them 'an unwholesome weed' which adulterated good ale. By the sixteenth century hop growing played an established part in farming, not only because of the flavour, but because of the preservative quality of hops.

Hop growing reached its peak in England in the nineteenth century, with the cultivation of over 70,000 acres (29,000 hectares) in 1878. The decline began in the early part of this century, though arrested for a while in the 1950s and 1960s. Since the 1970s the market for hops has again decreased, this time mainly as the result of competition from the USA and Europe. Technical

Traditional hop garden

developments at the brewing stage also mean that fewer hops are now required. Today less than 4,000 hectares are cultivated for hop growing. Continued research at Wye College in Kent helps to maintain a high standard in English hops. Since 1982 English Hops Ltd from Paddock Wood has organised the sale of hops to 90% of brewers in the UK. The hop still provides the ingredient that puts the 'bitter' in beer. No substitute, were it needed, has yet been found.

The South East of England, and Kent above all, has always been the chief area for hop growing and produces half the hops now grown. The other half comes from Hereford and Worcester.

Though now much automated, hop growing is still labour-intensive. Watch for the traditional seasonal activities - stringing in spring, with a long pole, twiddling in early summer as well as harvesting in early September.

WALKING ADVICE

No season of the year is closed to walkers; enjoyment can be gained from walking on a bright crisp winter's morning, or on an 'Indian summer's day' in the autumn. Equally rewarding is a springtime walk when the countryside is full of new life and growth.

Always wear suitable clothing and footwear for the season. Be prepared for changeable weather. Take with you clothes which are warm and waterproof. Inexpensive overtrousers will protect you from any discomfort caused by walking through high vegetation or crops after rain. Sections of the path may be muddy after periods of rain so wear strong, comfortable and waterproof footwear.

Allow plenty of time to complete your

chosen walk. Reckon on walking 2 or $2\frac{1}{2}$ miles an hour. The distances and times for each section of the walk are shown in the narrative text, and in the information. Allow more time if it has been wet, if you are elderly, or have children or inexperienced walkers with you.

The route has been established in consultation with landowners and farmers and follows public rights of way. Remember that most public paths cross private estates and farmland; they were developed as routes from farms to the nearest village, and were not designed for large numbers of people. You are walking through a place of work; enjoy the countryside but please show respect for its life and work. Crops and animals are the farmers' livelihood, so leave them alone.

Always keep to the path to avoid trespass. When faced with a growing crop you may have to seek a way round the edge of the field even though in law the landowner or farmer is supposed to keep the footpath clear. Walk in single file through a crop. In case you come across a path which has become overgrown, you will find it useful to carry secateurs to help clear the way. You may remove any obstruction on a right of way sufficiently to allow you to proceed.

Take care when crossing or walking along country roads. Keep to the right, in single file, facing oncoming traffic. On a bend, however, walk on the outside and keep a good lookout for traffic.

Remember to leave things as they are - refasten those gates you find closed. Straying stock can cause damage and an expensive inconvenience to farmers. If you find a gate open do not close it if this would isolate stock from its water. Always use gates and stiles to cross fences and hedges.

Take your litter home with you otherwise it can injure people and animals (including wildlife). Guard against all risk of fire, especially in dry weather. Picnicking is not permitted on private land; you only have a right of passage on a right of way.

To avoid injury or distress to farm animals and wildlife, keep your dogs under control at all times. If not on a lead they can run surprisingly long distances and consequently out of sight of the owner. Farmers have a right to shoot dogs found worrying animals.

USING THE GUIDEBOOK

The book is designed to be a practical guide to walking the Greensand Way in Kent in either direction. The route maps have been arranged in sequence in ten sections, from Limpsfield Chart to Hamstreet. When walking, therefore, from west to east the book is used in the conventional way, whilst the east to west route is read from the back of the book to the front.

By carefully folding it back, the book will fit into a map case, thus providing protection against damage, dirt and wetness.

Because the countryside is constantly changing, with stiles, gates, and field boundaries being removed or new ones erected, there are no route directions. Route finding should not be a problem given the large scale route maps and the extensive waymarking on the ground.

ROUTE MAP INFORMATION

The route maps are reproduced from the Ordnance Survey 1:10,000 series, reduced to a scale of $3^{1}/_{2}$" to the mile.

The maps are aligned north/south on each page, and run from west to east

throughout the book. For convenience the scale appears on some maps.

MAPS

Ordnance Survey sheet numbers and titles:

Landranger Series, scale 1:50,000 - 1 $^{1}/_{4}$" to the mile.
187 Dorking, Reigate and Crawley area
188 Maidstone & The Weald of Kent
189 Ashford & Romney Marsh area

Pathfinder Series, scale 1:25,000 - $2^{1}/_{2}$" to the mile.
1208 (TQ 45/55) Sevenoaks and Westerham
1209 (TQ 65/75) Maidstone
1229 (TQ 64/74) Paddock Wood and Staplehurst
1230 (TQ 84/94) Headcorn and Charing
1250 (TQ 83/93) Tenterden
1251 (TR 03) Aldington

DISTANCES AND TIME

The distances and times for each section of the walk are shown in the narrative text and in the information below.

GRID REFERENCES

Most of the interesting places and features along the Greensand Way have been given a grid reference in the narrative text.

The framework of squares spaced at one kilometre intervals over all Ordnance Survey maps is known as the National Grid. The grid facilitates the pinpointing of any place in the country giving it a unique reference number.

To give a reference number, first take the western (left-hand) edge of the kilometre square in which the place lies. Read the figures at the end of the line in the top and bottom margins of the map,

then moving eastwards (to the right) estimate the position of the place in tenths across the square. Secondly, take the southern edge of the same square and read the figures at the end of the line in the side margins of the map. Then, moving northwards, estimate the position of the place in tenths up the square. This gives the place a six figure reference number accurate to within 100 metres.

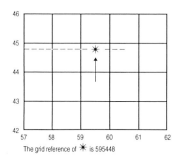

The grid reference of ✳ is 595448

In finding out a grid reference, the first three numbers of the six figure number refer to the line and number of tenths across the square, whilst the second three numbers refer to the line and number of tenths up the square.

PLANNING A WALK

The Greensand Way in Kent is 55 miles in length and can be undertaken as a long distance walk in three or more days. Westerham, the nearest town to the western end of the Kent section, is accessible by bus from Sevenoaks, Bromley and Reigate. A local service connects Limpsfield Chart and Oxted. Hamstreet at the eastern end is accessible by bus from Ashford and by train from Ashford, Rye and Hastings.

If you wish to undertake the Greensand Way in sections you need to be aware of problems of returning to your starting point. Possible solutions might be as follows:

a) Using two cars, one at the starting point and the other at the proposed finishing point;

b) Using one car and public transport. If relying on infrequent bus services it is suggested that you make your outward journey by bus thus returning confidently to your car or base;

c) Retracing your steps - the scenery can look surprisingly different when you are walking the other way.

The walk can be undertaken in sections as follows: (Included in the distances are the link paths to and from the access point shown in brackets).

Goodley Stock (Westerham) - Knole Park (Sevenoaks Bus Station): 13 $^{1}/_{4}$ miles, allow 6 $^{3}/_{4}$ hours. (bus link between Westerham and Sevenoaks).

Knole Park (Sevenoaks Railway Station) - Yalding (Railway Station): 13 miles, allow 6$^{1}/_{2}$ hours (rail link between Sevenoaks and Yalding, via Paddock Wood).

Yalding (Railway Station) - Pluckley (Railway Station): 20$^{1}/_{2}$ miles, allow 10 $^{1}/_{4}$ hours (rail link between Yalding and Pluckley, via Paddock Wood).

Pluckley (Railway Station) - Great Chart (Ashford Railway Station): 10 miles, allow 5 hours (rail link between Pluckley and Ashford).

Little Chart (Charing Railway Station) - Great Chart (Ashford Railway Station): 9$^{1}/_{2}$ miles, allow 4 $^{3}/_{4}$ hours (rail link between Charing and Ashford).

Great Chart (Ashford Railway Station) - Hamstreet (Railway Station): 8 miles, allow 4 hours (rail link between Ashford and Hamstreet).

You can devise shorter walks utilising the bus routes which link with various places along the route.

SIGNING AND WAYMARKING

Linear waymark

The Greensand Way logo and waymarks are used to show the line of the route in Kent. You will see them fixed to waymark posts, poles or posts of gates or stiles. The Way has been waymarked in such a way that it is possible for you to walk the route in either direction.

Please note that, at the request of Lord Sackville, the Sevenoaks route through Knole Park is waymarked with link path arrows only.

Greensand Way sign

Link path waymark

At regular points along the route you will see metal signs fixed to lamp posts or some other post. These show access to the route from towns, villages, railway stations and some bus routes, and display the logo and arrow coloured brown and white. The link paths are waymarked with specially adapted arrows with the words 'LINK PATH'

printed on them.

These access points and link paths will enable you to devise your own shorter walks utilising private and/or public transport.

In Surrey the waymarking consists of the letters GW printed onto yellow arrows.

TRANSPORT

Car Parking

Car parking places are shown on the route maps. Please note that these are not necessarily car parks. If a car park is not available, please park thoughtfully and sensibly to avoid causing an obstruction or damage to the roadside verges. Leave your car securely locked with valuables out of sight.

Bus and Train Services

It is not practical to give details of all the bus and train routes and services to and around the Greensand Way, since they may change during the currency of this guidebook. Both Kent and Surrey County Councils publish annual public transport guides, each which contain a comprehensive bus and rail route map and a list of bus services and operators (see below).

For details of train services, please telephone the following information offices:

For Ashford, Charing, Pluckley and Hamstreet, tel: Canterbury (0227) 454411. For Sevenoaks, Paddock Wood, Yalding, Oxted and Edenbridge, tel: Tonbridge (0732) 770111.

You are advised to check details of your journey before travelling, particularly with respect to Sunday services. Public Transport information countywide can be obtained from Kent Counry Council, Highways and Transportation

Department, Springfield, Maidstone, Kent ME14 2LX, tel: Maidstone (0622) 696996. Information on public transport in Surrey can be obtained from Surrey County Council, Transportation Planning Division, Highways and Transportation Department, Room 311, County Hall, Kingston-upon-Thames, Surrey KT1 2DN.

USEFUL ADDRESSES AND/OR TELEPHONE NUMBERS

If you have any comments or suggestions about this or any other recreation route, please contact the Access and Recreation Officer, Planning Department, Kent County Council, Springfield, Maidstone, Kent ME14 2LX, telephone Maidstone (0622) 696168.

The routes should not be obstructed in any way but if they are please contact the Public Rights of Way Manager, Highways & Transportation Department, Kent County Council, Springfield, Maidstone, Kent ME14 2LX, telephone Maidstone (0622) 696740.

Tourist Information
(including accommodation lists)

Edenbridge: Town Council Offices, Doggetts Barn, High Street, Edenbridge, Kent TN8 5AR, telephone Edenbridge (0732) 865368.

Sevenoaks: Tourist Information Centre, Buckhurst Lane, Sevenoaks, Kent TN13 1LQ, telephone Sevenoaks (0732) 450305.

Tonbridge: Tourist Information Centre, Tonbridge Castle, Castle Street, Tonbridge, Kent TN9 1BG, telephone Tonbridge (0732) 770929.

Maidstone: Tourist Information Centre, The Gatehouse, Old Palace Gardens, Mill Street, Maidstone, Kent ME15 6YE,

telephone Maidstone (0622) 673581.

Ashford: Tourist Information Centre, 18 Churchyard, Ashford, Kent TN23 1QG, telephone Ashford (0233) 629165.

Preservation Bodies
National Trust, Kent and East Sussex Regional Office, The Estate Office, Scotney Castle, Lamberhurst, Tunbridge Wells, Kent TN3 8JN, telephone Lamberhurst (0892) 890651.

English Heritage, London and South East Area Office, Spur 17, Government Buildings, Hawkenbury, Tunbridge Wells, Kent TN2 5AQ, telephone Tunbridge Wells (0892) 548166.

Historic Houses Association, 2 Chester Street, London SW1X 7BB, telephone (071-259) 5688.

Conservation Bodies
Kent Trust for Nature Conservation, Tyland Barn, Chatham Road, Sandling, Maidstone, Kent ME14 3BD, telephone (0622) 753017/759017.

English Nature, South East Regional Office, Countryside Management Centre, Coldharbour Farm, Wye, Ashford, Kent TN25 5DB, telephone Wye (0233) 812525.

Walkers' Organisations
Ramblers' Association, 1/5 Wandsworth Road, London SW8 2XX, telephone (071-582) 6878
Kent Area Secretary: Brian Arguile, 42 Waldron Drive, Loose, Maidstone, Kent ME15 9TH, telephone Maidstone (0622) 744207.

Long Distance Walkers' Association, Secretary: Alan Castle, Wayfarers, 9 Tainters Brook, Uckfield, East Sussex TN22 1UQ, telephone Uckfield (0825) 761803.
Kent Area Secretary: Mr D Sheldrake, 26

Highview, Vigo Village, Meopham, Gravesend, Kent DA13 ORR, telephone Fairseat (0732) 823643.

Youth Hostels Association, Trevelyan House, 8 St Stephens Hill, St Albans, Herts AL1 2DY, telephone St Albans (0727) 55215.

Miscellaneous
Countryside Commission, South East Regional Office, 4th floor, 71 Kingsway, London WC2B 6ST, telephone (071-831) 3510.

Ordnance Survey, Romsey Road, Maybush, Southampton, Hants SO9 4DH, telephone Southampton (0703) 792000.

Weatherdial (up-to-date weather forecast)
Inland Kent 0898 14 12 12
P & R Publicity Ltd
(Achievement Badges for most long distance paths), Queensway,

Mereworth (1 mile), Yalding, Hunton (1 ³/₄ miles), Linton, Loose (2 miles), Boughton Monchelsea (³/₄ mile), Wierton, Sutton Valence, East Sutton, Egerton, Pluckley, Charing (2¹/₂ miles by path), Hothfield (¹/₄ mile), Great Chart, Ashford (2 miles by path), Kingsnorth and Hamstreet.

Please telephone the Tourist Information Centres (listed elsewhere) for details.

For a copy of the Kent Accommodation Guide contact Kent Tourism, Economic Development Department, Kent County Council, Springfield, Maidstone, Kent ME14 2LX, telephone Maidstone (0622) 696165.

The Ramblers' Association (also listed) publishes the Ramblers' Year Book which contains an accommodation list. This book is available from local bookshops.

KEY TO MAP SYMBOLS

———	Greensand Way - fully signed and waymarked.	☎	Telephone
– – –	Link path (access point) fully signed and waymarked.	*i*	Tourist Information
• • • • •	Optional access point or detour to an interesting place or refreshments - not waymarked.	WC	Toilet
		🛏	Accommodation
SR242	Footpath number.	🍺	Public house
24	Interesting feature.	✗	Pub food
15	Miles from Surrey border (Limpsfield Chart)	❢❢❢	Cafe/restaurant
⇌	Railway station	🛆	Picnic site
🚌	Bus route		Foodstore
P	Car parking	☀	View point
		△	Caution - take care

You may join the YHA (also listed), on arrival at the hostel, but prior booking is advisable.

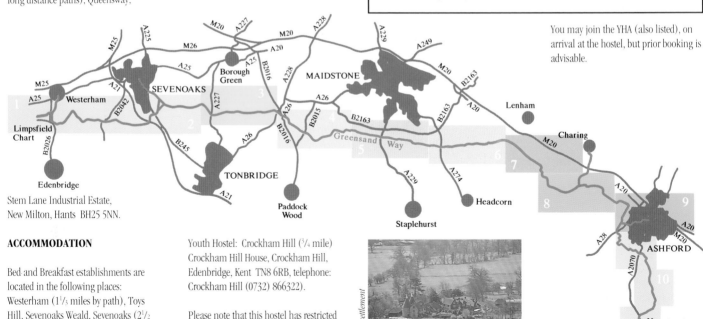

Wealden settlement

Stem Lane Industrial Estate, New Milton, Hants BH25 5NN.

ACCOMMODATION

Bed and Breakfast establishments are located in the following places: Westerham (1¹/₃ miles by path), Toys Hill, Sevenoaks Weald, Sevenoaks (2¹/₂ miles by path), Shipbourne, Plaxtol (1 mile), Hadlow (2 miles by path),

Youth Hostel: Crockham Hill (³/₄ mile) Crockham Hill House, Crockham Hill, Edenbridge, Kent TN8 6RB, telephone: Crockham Hill (0732) 866322).

Please note that this hostel has restricted opening arrangements and may close during the currency of this guidebook.

1

Limpsfield Chart - Brockhoult Mount
7 miles, allow 3 hours

Though strictly in the Surrey section of the Greensand Way, Limpsfield Chart (grid reference 425517) makes a good point to start or end your walk. The name Chart is a familiar one throughout Kent and particularly along the Greensand Way, appearing in such names as Chartwell, Great and Little Chart, Chart Sutton and several others.

The hurricane of 16 October 1987 brought down many trees of the Chart and of much of the Greensand ridge. You can now see where new growth is becoming established. To the north you can see the tops of the North Downs.

Goodley Stock
The narrow combe at Goodley Stock is typical of much of this part of the Greensand ridge where strong earth movements took place, with weathering. Its steep slopes are scattered with self-seeded rhododendron as well as birch, oak and rowan.

Remains of an Iron-Age fort (2) (grid reference 443522) stand on the eastern summit, opposite Goodley Stock. The most obvious entrance to Squerryes Park Camp is on the steep south-eastern side. The north-west of Kent has a number of sites such as this. The largest of these is at Oldbury Hill (grid reference 583565), near Ightham.

Kent Hatch
Kent Hatch (grid reference 439517),

meaning Kent Gate, is the most westerly point in Kent on the Greensand Way. The London-Lewes road as built by the Romans (1), or at least its probable alignment, runs across the Kent Hatch Road (grid reference 430517) but at this point it is in Surrey.

Crockhamhill Common (grid reference 444517) provides one of the many fine views of the Weald. Self-seeded foxgloves grow here, as well as rosebay willowherb and saxifrage. Bramble and bracken predominate.

Mariners Hill
Mariners Hill (grid reference 449513) is one of a number of National Trust properties in this area. Mariners Hill was partly given by Octavia Hill, a nineteenth-century pioneer social reformer and founder of the National Trust, between 1904 and 1908, partly bought by subscription in 1913. Octavia Hill lived in Crockham Hill. You can see her tombstone beside the path leading up to Holy Trinity Church (6) (grid reference 444507). Her effigy, showing an old lady in a shawl, is inside the church.

Chartwell
In the valley below Mariners Hill, to the east of the road, stands Chartwell (7) (grid reference 455515), well known as the home of Sir Winston Churchill. He bought it in 1924 and lived there until his death in 1965. From the path of the Greensand Way you can see the corner of the house and grounds through the trees. The house was bequeathed to the National Trust who display it much as the house was in the 1930s. The Victorian house was well-restored to reveal much of its Tudor origins. On view to the public are Second World War displays in the library, Churchill's study, paintings and porcelain.

Chartwell

French Street
An Iron Age coin hoard was found in a gravel workings above French Street (grid reference 456524). The fourteen gold staters, known as the Westerham gold, were probably hidden there by Celtic people.

The square oasts of French Street Farm (grid reference 460527) make a variation on the familiar conical form, a reminder of the time when much of the area bore hops. The square design dates from the early nineteenth century. Note the unusual octagonal cowls.

French Street Nursery (grid reference 464517) was formerly the kitchen garden and Italian water garden of Weardale Manor (grid reference 468522), a large house built on Toys Hill in 1906 by Lord Weardale of the Stanhope family. Weardale was demolished in 1940. A clump of pines marks where it stood. You can see the

imported conifers and the traces of the drive and lodge (8) (grid reference 470519).

Toys Hill
At 245 metres, Toys Hill (grid reference 468518) makes the highest point in Kent along the Greensand ridge. Leith Hill in Surrey is the highest overall. You can see as far as Haslemere (the western end of the Greensand Way in Surrey) in the south-west, and to Ashdown Forest in the south.

Toys Hill, part of the parish of Brasted, was common land from early times, used by swineherds who grazed their pigs on acorns. The woodland only grew up after the land of Brasted Chart was enclosed by Act of Parliament in 1853. The trees, pollarded to provide fresh

growth above the level reached by greedy snouts, pre-date the enclosure. The coppiced trees date from after that time, when it was possible to grow fresh timber at near-ground level.

Toys Hill, together with Ide Hill, suffered severe damage during the hurricane of 1987 to the extent that the landscape

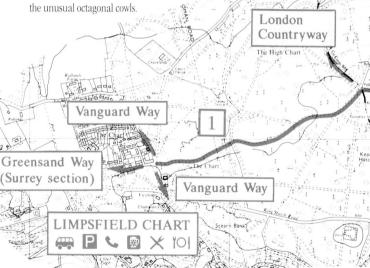

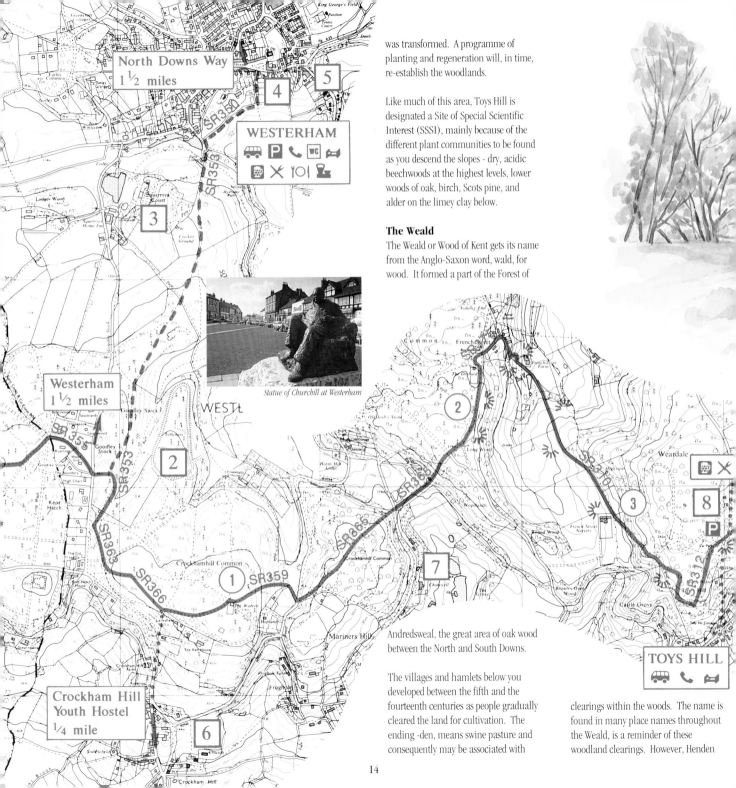

North Downs Way
1 ½ miles

【4】 【5】

WESTERHAM

【3】

Statue of Churchill at Westerham

Westerham
1 ½ miles

WEST

【2】

French Street

②

Weardale

③ 【8】

SR312

【7】

TOYS HILL

Crockham Hill
Youth Hostel
¼ mile

【6】

① SR359

was transformed. A programme of planting and regeneration will, in time, re-establish the woodlands.

Like much of this area, Toys Hill is designated a Site of Special Scientific Interest (SSSI), mainly because of the different plant communities to be found as you descend the slopes - dry, acidic beechwoods at the highest levels, lower woods of oak, birch, Scots pine, and alder on the limey clay below.

The Weald

The Weald or Wood of Kent gets its name from the Anglo-Saxon word, wald, for wood. It formed a part of the Forest of Andredsweal, the great area of oak wood between the North and South Downs.

The villages and hamlets below you developed between the fifth and the fourteenth centuries as people gradually cleared the land for cultivation. The ending -den, means swine pasture and consequently may be associated with clearings within the woods. The name is found in many place names throughout the Weald, is a reminder of these woodland clearings. However, Henden

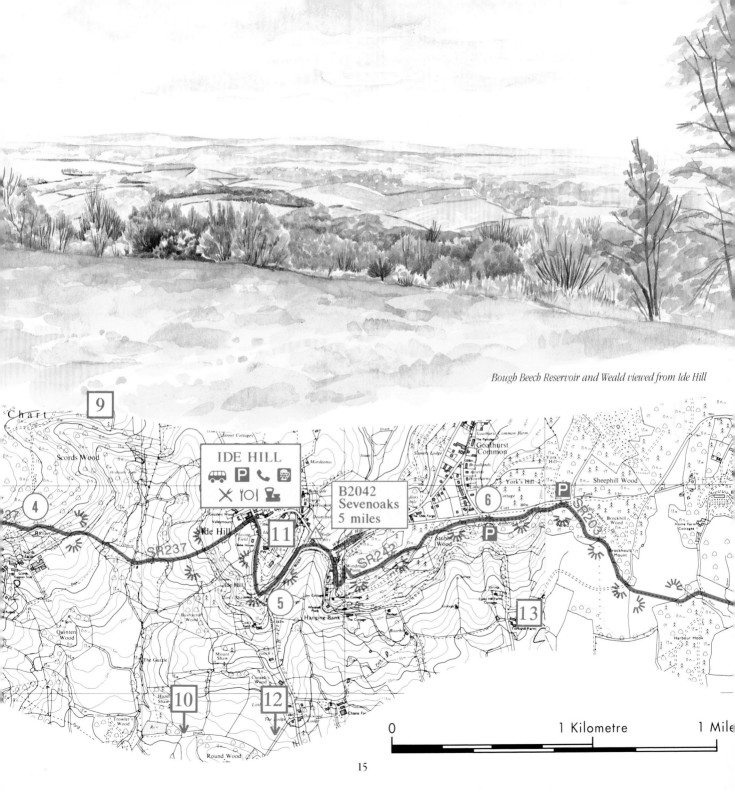

Bough Beech Reservoir and Weald viewed from Ide Hill

IDE HILL

B2042
Sevenoaks
5 miles

0   1 Kilometre   1 Mile

Emmetts Garden

(high clearing) at Henden Manor (10) (grid reference 483584), which you can make out on the spur south-west of Toys Hill, is better known as a place where Henry VIII stayed when visiting Anne Boleyn at Hever.

Bough Beech Reservoir

The large expanse of water to the south of the Greensand Way is Bough Beech Reservoir (12) (grid reference 495480). Completed in 1969, this fills a small tributary valley of the River Eden. Now the site offers fishing and sailing. It is also a valuable Nature Reserve, run by the Kent Trust for Nature Conservation.

The Octavia Hill Woodlands (grid reference 474522) were acquired by the National Trust through a special appeal in 1981. This was their last acquisition to make up the area owned here by them. The area includes Scords Wood (grid reference 477521), part of the SSSI, where you will find the same sequence of plant communities as at Toys Hill. On the acidic soil of the plateau you find beech, sessile and pedunculate oak, birch, whitebeam and rowan. In the lower woods pedunculate oak predominates, with bramble, wood sorrel, honeysuckle and wood anemone in the ground flora. Lower down, where lime is present in the soil, you find field maple, wild cherry and hazel in the canopy, while on the wet, alkaline soil of the wealden clay you see the guelder rose

joining the tree canopy and bugle, dog's mercury and wood-sedge mixing with nettles and nightshade in the undergrowth.

The square, grey house on the hillside to the north is Emmetts (9) (grid reference 488525), so-named because of the ants, for whom emmet is an old English name, who colonised the hillside. The gardens contain an outstanding collection of rhododendrons, azaleas and maples. The woods are carpeted with bluebells in spring. You can reach the entrance in about twenty minutes walk from Ide Hill.

Ide Hill

Ide Hill (grid reference 485515) grew up in the Middle Ages as a clearing on the old drovers' road from Brasted to Hever. The church (11) (grid reference 486517), whose spire stands prominently above the village, was built in 1865. It replaced an earlier chapel, even then only built in 1807. Before that, villagers walked to church in Sundridge.

The steep slope of Hanging Bank (grid reference 488544) illustrates the landslips that occur from time to time along the escarpment.

The slopes to the east of Ide Hill, Stubbs Wood (grid reference 495518) and Brockhill Wood, with Brockhoult Mount (grid reference 504518) lower down the

slope, are further Sites of Special Scientific Interest. As you walk along Lady Amhurst's Drive you may see sessile oak, pedunculate oak, birch, whitebeam and rowan among other trees of the plateau. As you go down the steep path you may find more pedunculate oak. The ground plants will include wood sorrel, honeysuckle and wood anemone.

Wealden Houses

Tucked into the hillside on the spur sloping down below Stubbs Wood lies Yorkshill Farm (13) (grid reference 497514), a converted Wealden hall-house. In medieval times, the typical Wealden house was built round a central hall, open from the ground floor to the roof. Smoke from the fire simply dispersed through cracks in the covering of the roof.

INTERESTING FEATURES

1 Roman Road
The course of a Roman road which ran between London (Londinivm) and Lewes in East Sussex.

2 Hill Fort and Settlement
A roughly triangular Iron Age fort of eleven acres defended by banks and ditches. An entrance was situated in the south-east corner.

WESTERHAM

3 Squerryes Court
A beautiful William and Mary Manor house acquired in 1735 by the Warde family who still live there today.

4 St Mary's Church
The 13th-century tower has a timber spiral staircase and a short shingle spire. It has a Perpendicular font and the Royal Arms of Edward VI.

5 Quebec House
A 17th-century red-brick gabled house with Tudor origins where General Wolfe, one of England's greatest soldiers, spent his early years.

6 Holy Trinity Church, Crockham Hill
A Victorian church built in 1842 by Charles Warde. Within, is a monument to Octavia Hill, a co-founder of the National Trust.

7 Chartwell
The home of Sir Winston Churchill from 1924 until his death, the rooms left as they were during his lifetime.

8 Weardale Lodge
The extant lodge of a now demolished house built on Toys Hill in 1906 by Lord Weardale of the Stanhope family.

9 Emmetts Garden
A five-acre hillside garden, one of the highest in Kent, noted for its fine new and rare trees and shrubs.

10 Hendon Manor
It is here that Henry VIII stayed when visiting Anne Boleyn at Hever Castle.

11 St Mary's Church, Ide Hill
A small Victorian church built in 1865-6 of ragstone with galleting.

12 Bough Beech Reservoir
Occupying a small tributary valley of the River Eden, the lake is used for recreation and is a water habitat for specialised flora and fauna.

13 Yorkshill Farm
A very big Wealden hall-house, built in 1476, with a traceried window remaining inside and a separate kitchen.

2

Brockhoult Mount - Cinderfield Wood
6 miles, allow 3 hours

Between Brockhill Wood and Sevenoaks Weald the Greensand Way takes you across rich farmland. You are still on relatively high ground, but the soil here is now clay. Watch here for signs of some of the changes taking place in British farming, such as the remains of an old hedge line (grid reference 505515), as farmers open up fields for wider acreage.

Wickhurst Manor (14) (grid reference 517513) was originally a Wealden hall-house with the mainly nineteenth-century house built around the hall. The outer walls include a fifteenth-century stone doorway.

From the top of the slope just east of Dale Farm (grid reference 527513) you will see higher, wooded slopes to the north and north-east. To the north-east is Hubbards Hill (grid reference 529523), east of that Beechmont Bank (grid reference 536524). These slopes, on the crest of the escarpment, were formed by solifluction, a process by which thawed soil moved downwards over frozen ground in cold areas. Slopes below these hills are the lobes formed by the debris.

Sevenoaks Weald

The Church of St George at Sevenoaks Weald (15) (grid reference 529513) was built, like the village, in the nineteenth century, as people discovered the attractions of living in the Weald, away from the main towns. The nave and the tower of St George were built in 1820, the chancel in 1872, all in Portland stone.

Riverhill House (16) (grid reference 543522) on the slope overlooking the Weald, has fine gardens created in the mid nineteenth century. Here John Rogers, one of the first members of the Royal Horticultural Society, established plants and shrubs then new to the country. The acid soil was ideal for their introduction. Cedars of Lebanon, deodar cedars and a wellingtonia as well as azaleas and rhododendron flourish here.

Parkland flora

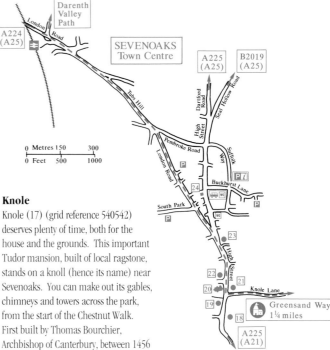

Knole

Knole (17) (grid reference 540542) deserves plenty of time, both for the house and the grounds. This important Tudor mansion, built of local ragstone, stands on a knoll (hence its name) near Sevenoaks. You can make out its gables, chimneys and towers across the park, from the start of the Chestnut Walk. First built by Thomas Bourchier, Archbishop of Canterbury, between 1456 and 1486, it was enlarged by Henry VIII. Queen Elizabeth later gave it to her cousin Thomas Sackville, whose descendants still live here. The house contains a unique collection of rare and important seventeenth-century furniture and textiles. There are paintings by Reynolds and cartoons by Raphael.

The one-thousand-acre Park is classed as an SSSI. It contains pollarded oaks which may survive from the wildwood. The tops of the trees were cut off so as to produce close rounded heads of young branches. Extensive grazing by the deer in the park has prevented a good shrub layer from forming and so limited the growth of trees, but the dead wood supports important fungus and lichen. This is also host to the best collection of invertebrates in Kent.

One Tree Hill

At 206 metres One Tree Hill (grid reference 561532) gives another outstanding view of the Weald with the scarp face dropping almost sheer in places. Ancient trees still exist here, among those of newer origin. Look for the familiar plateau species here - sessile oak, birch, whitebeam, beech, hazel with undergrowth of hawthorn, blackthorn and elder. On the slopes you will also find ash and a few wych elms which survived the Dutch Elm disease. This is a place for firsts, the only place in Kent where you might find the bristletail snail, and the only place the slug tandonia rustica has been sighted.

In the woods below Shingle Hill (grid reference 569532) you will see bluebells in spring, and golden saxifrage where the ground is wetter.

As you walk you will see a number of landmarks. To the south- east you can see the tower of St Giles Church at Shipbourne (26) (grid reference 592522) (pronounced Shibbon). You can also see from a distance Fairlawne House (27) (grid reference 595534)

Knole, house and deer park

three-quarters of a mile north of Shipbourne.

INTERESTING FEATURES

14 Wickhurst Manor
Embedded in the 19th-century house is a medieval hall with a crown post roof. The masonry of the centre of the south front belongs to this.

15 St George's Church, Sevenoaks Weald
The nave and the tower were built in 1820 and the chancel in 1872. The interior of the chancel glows with stencilled designs.

16 Riverhill House
A small country house, the home of the Rogers family since 1840. It contains panelled rooms, portraits and memorabilia.

SEVENOAKS

17 Knole
A large house dating from 1456 and enlarged in 1603 by Thomas Sackville, first Earl of Dorset, to whom it was granted by Queen Elizabeth I.

18 Sevenoaks School and Almshouses
A school for free education of poor children was founded in 1432. It was rebuilt in 1724-32 and is now a public school. The almshouses and school are of the same period.

19 The Chantry
Dating from 1700, the house recalls in its name a small farm with which a 13th-century rector endowed his gift of a chantry in the church.

20 St Nicholas' Church
Established in the 12th century, the church, which possesses features in all gothic styles, was enlarged in the 15th century.

SEVENOAKS WEALD

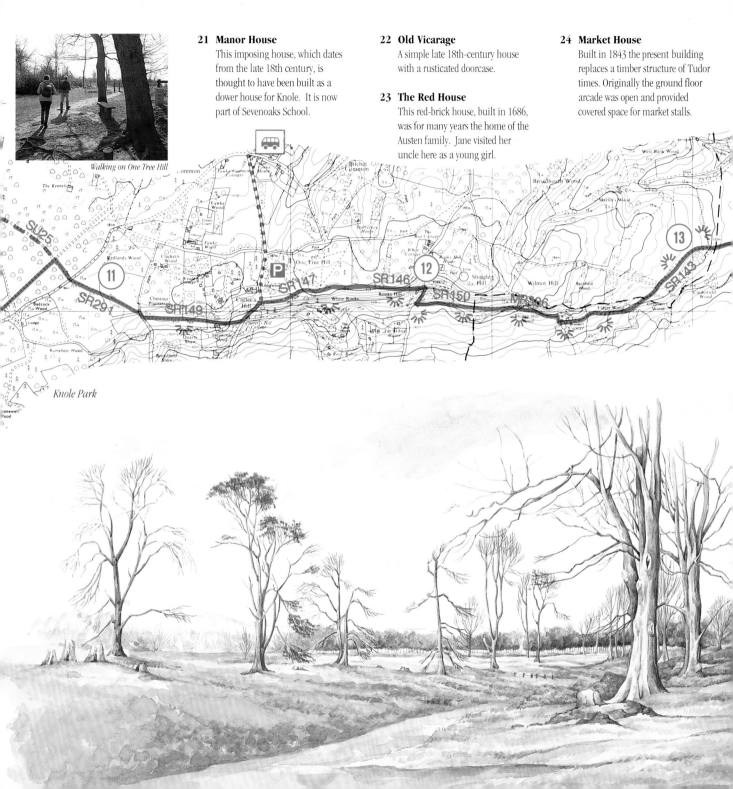

21 Manor House
This imposing house, which dates from the late 18th century, is thought to have been built as a dower house for Knole. It is now part of Sevenoaks School.

22 Old Vicarage
A simple late 18th-century house with a rusticated doorcase.

23 The Red House
This red-brick house, built in 1686, was for many years the home of the Austen family. Jane visited her uncle here as a young girl.

24 Market House
Built in 1843 the present building replaces a timber structure of Tudor times. Originally the ground floor arcade was open and provided covered space for market stalls.

Walking on One Tree Hill

Knole Park

3

Cinderfield Wood - Forge Farm
5½ miles, allow 2¾ hours

Ightham Mote

Ightham Mote (25) (grid reference 584534) is one of the finest surviving moated manor houses in the country. Started soon after 1340, the first recorded owner was Sir Thomas Cawne in 1360. By 1530 it had a great hall, chapel, crypt and two solars. Later came a

sixteenth-century chapel, a Jacobean drawing room and many Victorian additions. Ightham Mote is undergoing extensive repairs but is open to the public who may see the conservation work in action.

The name Ightham possibly refers to attackers (Old English ehtan, meaning to persecute or attack), but this was a peaceful place in recorded history. The name 'Mote' refers to the moot or council which used to meet there.

Half a mile north you will find Ivy Hatch (grid reference 587544). The name Hatch meant a high gate leading to a forest. Ivy Hatch was the junction of a number of ancient trackways which led through the Wealden forest to the main route, later known as the Pilgrims' Way, along the edge of the North Downs.

Shipbourne (pronounced 'Shibbon') St Giles' Church (26) (grid reference 592522) is Early English in style but it was rebuilt, first by James Gibbs in 1721-2, then by Edward Cazalet in 1880-81. If the church is open look at the carving and bright wall stencilling inside. The other features include a stone carved pulpit and a splendid monument to the first Lord Barnard and his lady, with their daughter reclining at their feet.

Tortoise-shell butterfly

Outside St Giles' Church, look up at the gargoyles which wing their way from the four corners of the tower. At the gateway note the coffin rest in the centre of the lych-gate.

Two literary connections link Shipbourne with the wider world of their times. Sir Henry Vane, owner of the old Fair Lane house, is buried in the vault of St Giles. He was executed on Tower Hill by Charles II for supporting the Roundheads. Samuel Pepys observed the execution. Christopher Smart, classical scholar and poet, was born in Shipbourne in 1722. He wrote a lengthy poem in blank verse, 'The Hop Garden'. He later became mad but apparently in an endearing way, with religious mania. Dr Johnson said of him 'I'd as soon pray with Kit Smart as anyone'.

As you cross the Green at Shipbourne you will see various examples of hung tiles traditional throughout Kent, on the upper walls of houses old and new. The sloping farmland below and around the immaculate stone buildings of Fairlawne Home Farm (grid reference 603524) was part of the Fairlawne estate.

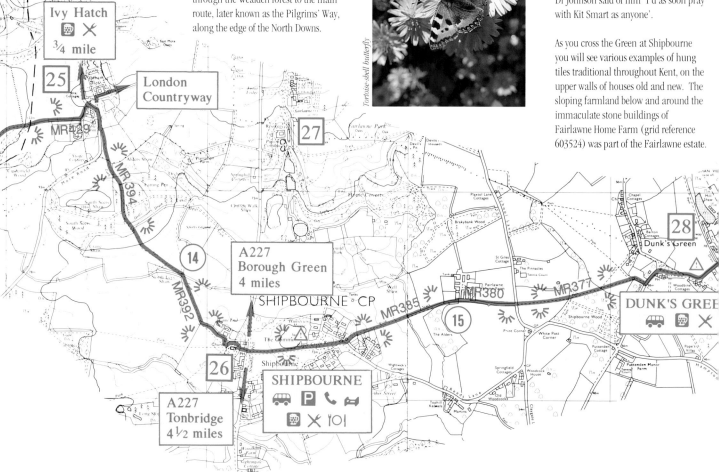

Ightham Mote

WEST PECKHAM

Wealdway

Wealdway

0   1 Kilometre   1 Mile

Fairlawne House

An older house on the site, which was a moated manor, used to be called Fair Lane, suggesting that the medieval fair took place here at one time. The present house was built of ragstone in the early eighteenth century. It has Tuscan columns, a belfry and cupola, added in the mid-1800s. Fairlawne House was the home of the Cazalets from 1872. Major Peter Cazalet became trainer of racehorses to HM the Queen Mother.

Many Palaeolithic artifacts, a Bronze Age axe and Iron Age pottery have been found along the Bourne, a tributary of the Medway, which flows through Roughway (grid reference 615527). One of two Roman villas in the area (grid reference 613531) yielded a fine statue of Minerva. From the early nineteenth century the Mill (28) (grid reference 616529) beside the Bourne produced high quality paper, including paper for stamps, bank notes and postal orders.

Hamptons (30) (grid reference 622522) stands on a spur running south-east from the Greensand Way. It was built in 1813, in stone-dressed yellow brick, in classical style. You can see the stable block with its white cupola to the east. The designer was R W Jearrad who later designed much at Cheltenham.

West Peckham Church

Oxen Hoath

The house, Oxen Hoath (31) (grid reference 631521), visible in winter after leaf-fall, reveals a curious mixture of styles and influences. Late eighteenth or early nineteenth century, its main material is traditional ragstone but you will see a French-style dome over the bow of the roof line, a white cornice all round and pediments rising from the windows below, all added sometime in the eighteen-forties. The house was once owned by the Geary family who were buried in West Peckham church. The Colepepers also lived there.

West Peckham

The church and village green of West Peckham (32) (grid reference 645525) are tucked away at the end of a side

Village Green, West Peckham

road. St Dunstan's Church, of ragstone and with a low tower and four-sided spire, is said to date from Saxon times. Especially interesting is the first-floor chapel on the north-east. Sir John Colepeper, a judge, founded this in 1408 as a chantry for daily prayers for Henry IV. It later became the private pew for the Geary family, owners of Oxen Hoath. Note especially the late seventeenth-century carved doorway to the pew and the nine hatchments of the Geary family on the ceiling.

On the corner at the east of the village is Duke's Place (33) (grid reference 648527), a large, half-timbered house of the early fifteenth century. It stands on land which Sir John Colepeper granted to the Knights Hospitallers of the Order of St John in 1337 and may have been the local Commandery until the Order was dissolved in 1540 by Henry VIII. The Order of the Knights Hospitallers was founded during the time of the Crusades to care for the sick and wounded and to look after Christian pilgrims going to Jerusalem.

INTERESTING FEATURES

25 Ightham Mote

A beautiful medieval moated manor house with its original great hall, chapel and crypt of c.1340, together with important later additions.

26 St Giles' Church, Shipbourne

Rebuilt in 1722 on medieval foundations and again in 1880, the church contains a monument to first Lord and Lady Barnard sculptured by Rysbrack and notable wall stencilling.

27 Fairlawne

This ragstone house, built in the early 18th century, was the home of the Cazalet family from 1872.

28 Roughway Mills

From the early 19th century the mill beside the Bourne produced high quality paper for postal and currency use.

29 Old Soar Manor

The remains of a late 13th-century Knights' manor house, comprising the two-storey solar and chapel.

30 Hamptons

A yellow-brick built house of 1813 with stone dressings. A central porch has two pairs of Greek Ionic columns. The house was gutted by fire in 1883.

31 Oxen Hoath

A late 18th-century, early 19th-century ragstone house with a highly bizarre roof line.

Detail of Ightham Mote

32 St Dunstan's Church, West Peckham

The medieval church has a Saxon tower and inside a remarkable family pew for the owners of Oxen Hoath.

33 Dukes Place

A large half-timbered house dating from the early 15th century and built on land granted to the Knights Hospitallers in 1337.

4

Forge Farm - Barn Hill Farm
6½ miles, allow 3¼ hours

The large red-brick house clearly visible from the slopes to the east of West Peckham is seventeenth-century Yotes Court (34) (grid reference 651534). The name 'Yotes', linked with 'yoke', refers to the amount of land which could be ploughed by a pair of yoked oxen.

The spire of St Lawrence's Church, Mereworth (grid reference 666538) is visible to the north. This was built in the eighteenth century when the Earl of Westmorland had the church moved five-eighths of a mile from its old position. He based the design on a mixture of famous London churches. The steeple is a replica of Gibbs' St Martin-in-the-Fields.

At the small footbridge over the stream (grid reference 653524) below Forge Farm you will hear the sound of water falling over an old brick dam. The dam created fish ponds (35) (grid reference 654528) for Yotes Court.

As you walk along the bridleway which runs between Forge Farm (grid reference 656524) and four converted oasts, three round and one square, bear in mind that this, not the A26 above, was once the main London Road. Forge Farm was a public house, the house below it a public house too, though at an earlier time. The forge itself, which served the farm there, was situated in the low barn-like building at the end. The half-timbered house on the south side was a Wealden hall-house.

The B2016, known as Seven Mile Lane, was built in the early nineteenth century to speed the transport of much-needed iron from the Weald to the Thames.

Twyford Bridge at Yalding

St Michael's Church
St Michael's Church (36) (grid reference 662522) now maintained by the Redundant Churches Fund, stands on the probable site of the early village of East Peckham. The later and modern village is some three miles to the south beside the River Medway. Note the weather-boarded shed by the gate built as a stable for parishioners attending services. Some of the stalls and stallholders' names survive. There are fine views over the Weald which you can enjoy from the seat placed outside the gate.

Three miles to the south-east you can make out the white cowls of thirty two conical oasts. These were built in 1812, in the heyday of the hop industry. They belong to the Whitbread Hop Farm (grid reference 673474) at Beltring.

Roydon Hall
Roydon Hall (37) (grid reference 666517) lies in the hollow a third of a mile below East Peckham church. The north and east fronts date from about 1870, but the west front is sixteenth century. It has impressive brick crow stepped gables, and Jacobean chimneys.

Early owners include the Twysden family, of whom Sir Roger Twysden was a keen Royalist Pamphleteer and, for a while in the Civil Wars, a prisoner of the

Parliamentarians in a hulk on the Thames. Roydon Hall's claim to be the 'Home of the Enlightenment in England' is made by the international transcendental meditation movement who now own it.

River Medway
By the stile between Moat Wood and the arable fields (grid reference 674513), you see the land gradually sloping downhill as it forms the Medway Valley. The River Medway flows north-eastwards to Maidstone and then past Rochester, to join the Thames at Sheerness. It rises as a spring in the Tunbridge Wells Sands above Turners Hill near East Grinstead in the Ashdown Forest. A catchment river for the many smaller rivers which drain water off the impermeable clay slopes of the Weald, the Medway used in times of heavy rainfall to cause serious flooding in the area near Yalding. A flood storage area above Tonbridge now controls this.

The Medway was important from Roman times onward for the transport of iron from the Weald and of ragstone from the Greensand ridge downstream to the Thames. Now the National Rivers Authority manages it for water extraction. The NRA also controls pollution and manages it for conservation, as an amenity and for navigation.

Hampstead Lock (grid reference 686504) is the deepest of the ten locks along the Medway Navigation. This covers nineteen miles of the freshwater Medway between Allington Lock, below Maidstone, and Tonbridge.

Hampstead Lane (grid reference 688503) takes you beside Hampstead Cut, a canal which links two points on the Medway to avoid the loop in the river. The canal was built in the mid eighteenth century by the Medway Navigation Company to

meet ever increasing demands to transport iron and timber from the Weald downstream to the Thames.

The Lees (grid reference 694499) was, until this century, common land owned by the Lord of the Manor. Originally formed by alluvium deposited by Medway floodings and consequently very marshy, it was drained as the water table was lowered.

The River Beult flows westwards from the Hythe Sandstone ridge to form the longest tributary of the Medway. The River Teise rises just east of Frant, near Tunbridge Wells. Like all Wealden rivers, the Teise responds very rapidly to rainfall, traditionally becoming a torrent in times of heavy downpours. The poet Edmund Blunden (1896-1974), whose father was a master at the National School in Yalding, describes its 'Deep foaming floods and foaming flocks of whirlwaves' (from 'To Teise a stream in Kent'). Now three flow gauging stations help to control the water.

Yalding
Both bridges in Yalding are medieval. Twyford Bridge (38) (grid reference 691498), the 'Bridge of the two fords', with brick refuges and pointed cutwaters, spans the Medway. The Town Bridge (39) (grid reference 697490) spans the

Thatched cottage at Yalding

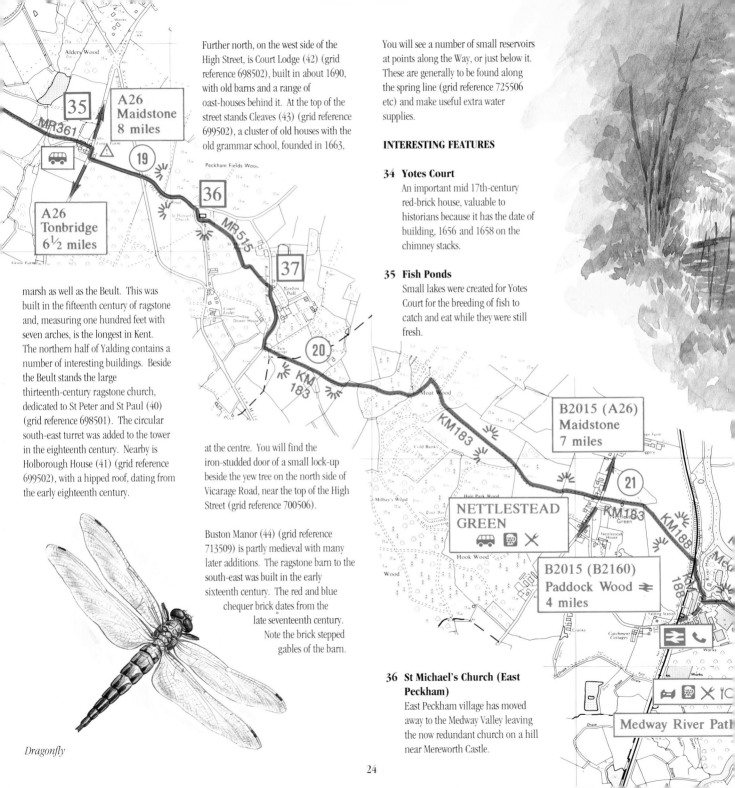

Further north, on the west side of the High Street, is Court Lodge (42) (grid reference 698502), built in about 1690, with old barns and a range of oast-houses behind it. At the top of the street stands Cleaves (43) (grid reference 699502), a cluster of old houses with the old grammar school, founded in 1663,

marsh as well as the Beult. This was built in the fifteenth century of ragstone and, measuring one hundred feet with seven arches, is the longest in Kent. The northern half of Yalding contains a number of interesting buildings. Beside the Beult stands the large thirteenth-century ragstone church, dedicated to St Peter and St Paul (40) (grid reference 698501). The circular south-east turret was added to the tower in the eighteenth century. Nearby is Holborough House (41) (grid reference 699502), with a hipped roof, dating from the early eighteenth century.

Dragonfly

at the centre. You will find the iron-studded door of a small lock-up beside the yew tree on the north side of Vicarage Road, near the top of the High Street (grid reference 700506).

Buston Manor (44) (grid reference 713509) is partly medieval with many later additions. The ragstone barn to the south-east was built in the early sixteenth century. The red and blue chequer brick dates from the late seventeenth century. Note the brick stepped gables of the barn.

36 St Michael's Church (East Peckham)
East Peckham village has moved away to the Medway Valley leaving the now redundant church on a hill near Mereworth Castle.

You will see a number of small reservoirs at points along the Way, or just below it. These are generally to be found along the spring line (grid reference 725506 etc) and make useful extra water supplies.

INTERESTING FEATURES

34 Yotes Court
An important mid 17th-century red-brick house, valuable to historians because it has the date of building, 1656 and 1658 on the chimney stacks.

35 Fish Ponds
Small lakes were created for Yotes Court for the breeding of fish to catch and eat while they were still fresh.

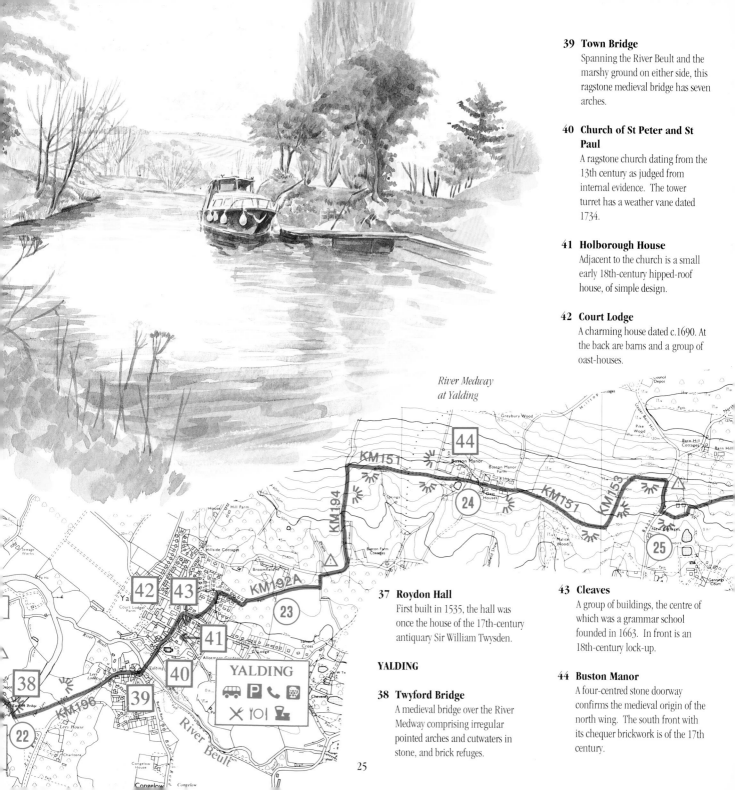

River Medway at Yalding

39 Town Bridge
Spanning the River Beult and the marshy ground on either side, this ragstone medieval bridge has seven arches.

40 Church of St Peter and St Paul
A ragstone church dating from the 13th century as judged from internal evidence. The tower turret has a weather vane dated 1734.

41 Holborough House
Adjacent to the church is a small early 18th-century hipped-roof house, of simple design.

42 Court Lodge
A charming house dated c.1690. At the back are barns and a group of oast-houses.

37 Roydon Hall
First built in 1535, the hall was once the house of the 17th-century antiquary Sir William Twysden.

YALDING

38 Twyford Bridge
A medieval bridge over the River Medway comprising irregular pointed arches and cutwaters in stone, and brick refuges.

43 Cleaves
A group of buildings, the centre of which was a grammar school founded in 1663. In front is an 18th-century lock-up.

44 Buston Manor
A four-centred stone doorway confirms the medieval origin of the north wing. The south front with its chequer brickwork is of the 17th century.

5

Barn Hill Farm - Chart Hill
5¼ miles, allow 2½ hours

Linton

Linton (grid reference 754502) is the westernmost of a line of villages running along the edge of the escarpment which may originally have formed a pilgrim route to Canterbury.

St Nicholas' Church (45) (grid reference 754502) built in ragstone in the Perpendicular style, contains one of the best collections of monuments you will

Bluebells

find. Do not miss the one in the north aisle to Sir Anthony Mayne and his two wives.

and the South Downs. Below is a park where fallow deer have wandered for three hundred years. The present ragstone house was built from 1567 onwards on the site of a medieval manor house. The battlements were only installed in 1819. The name Boughton, pronounced Borton, comes from Bocton, meaning a clearing in a beech wood, Monchelsea from the Monchensies, a Norman family who held the land in the twelfth century.

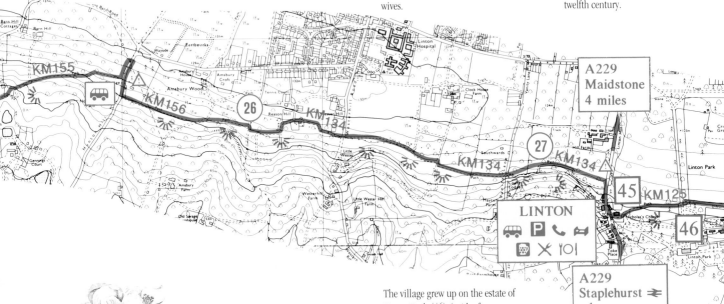

The village grew up on the estate of Linton Park (46) (grid reference 758499) where Robert Mann first built his huge house in 1730. You can see the north facade down a long avenue as you walk to the east of the church. This side has two storeys but the south, clinging to the scarp slope has three. In white stucco and with Corinthian columns, it prompted Horace Walpole, a friend of Robert Mann, to call it 'that citadel of Kent with the Weald as its garden'.

Boughton Monchelsea

Boughton Monchelsea Place (48) (grid reference 771499) is another house set in a dramatic position on the edge of the escarpment. From here you can see Tenterden church, Goudhurst, Benenden

The first owner of the present house was Robert Rudston who went to the Tower for taking part in Wyatt's rebellion in 1554, just after buying it. He repurchased the house on his release. You can visit it between Easter and early October and see the Elizabethan staircase, a late seventeenth-century staircase, eighteenth-century mock Gothic pillars in the hall and a Regency dining room in a house continuously occupied since it was first built.

St Peter's Church (47) (grid reference 771499) stands in the southern corner of the garden. Much of this was rebuilt in

Apple blossom

the nineteenth century after a fire in 1832, but further work in the 1870s reused old Perpendicular windows and some traces of the original Norman church. The medieval lych-gate, with a crown-post roof, is claimed to be the oldest in England.

In the churchyard you can see some of the ways people have chosen to remember their families. They include a mausoleum, some table tombs, a line of body tombs and a headstone showing a man jumping from his coffin at the sound of the last trump. In the last, look also for the angel of life, the broken scythe and the skeleton. Another headstone records a miracle when Sarah Tomkins had her sight restored after twelve years of blindness.

INTERESTING FEATURES

45 St Nicholas' Church, Linton
This plain and restored Victorian Church contains an interesting collection of monuments to members of the Mayne and Mann families.

46 Linton Park
Robert Mann's 1730's house was enlarged c.1829 by Thomas Cubitt. The treatment of the exterior is reminiscent of Carlton House Terrace.

Linton

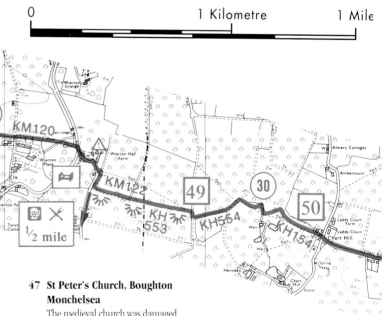

Boughton Monchelsea Place

47 St Peter's Church, Boughton Monchelsea
The medieval church was damaged by fire in 1832 and rebuilt in 1874. Notable is the lych-gate which is wholly medieval.

48 Boughton Monchelsea Place
An L-shaped ragstone house, the east range of which is Tudor, whilst the remainder was rebuilt c.1819 with battlements.

49 Roman Road
The probable alignment of a Roman road which ran between Rochester (Dvrobrivae) and Bodiam in East Sussex.

6

Chart Hill - Elmstone Hole Road
5 miles, allow 2½ hours

Ladds Court (50) (grid reference 795495) is an interesting mixture of styles with close-studded timbering to the west front and Georgian red brick on the south.

Chart Sutton

In the Middle Ages a settlement covered a strip of land running north to south down the ridge. This pattern is seen in many other villages along the Way. The

Sutton Valence Castle

Sutton Valence

Sutton Valence, once held by the Valence family, is a small hill-town, perched on the edge of the escarpment. Its terraced roads follow the contours of the hillside. The school was founded in 1576 by William Lambe, a wealthy clothmaker.

Lambe is also remembered in the name of Lambe's Conduit Street in Holborn, where he brought water to the people of the area in 1577. A row of almshouses, founded by him in 1580, stands in the High Street.

Church of St Michael (51) (grid reference 804494) was built at different times, on the site of an earlier Saxon church. The ragstone tower dates from the fourteenth century. A mounting block stands beside the gate. Note the shaped gables on the red and grey chequer brick granary.

In St Mary's Churchyard (52) (grid reference 810492) you can see the tombstone of John Willes (1777-1852), the cricketer who introduced round-arm bowling.

The portion of the lane to the north of St Mary's Church before it meets the

mainroad, is part of the Roman road (53) which ran from Maidstone via Kingsnorth to Lympne. This was one of several wealdways which linked up with the main Roman roads, such as Watling Street. From Sutton Valence this road descended to the Weald, down the side of the escarpment. Sutton Valence Castle (55) (grid reference 815492) was later built beside it by the Normans.

East Sutton

The prison at East Sutton (58) (grid reference 830497) provided a dramatic scene during the Civil Wars. The seventeenth-century owner of East Sutton Park (56) (grid reference 826494), Sir Robert Filmer, was a friend of Charles I and declared his support for the king by writing 'a Book of the Divine Right of Kings'. He was besieged in the house by General Fairfax and the Parliamentarians, eventually captured and then imprisoned in Leeds Castle.

The Church of St Peter and St Paul (57) (grid reference 828495), mainly thirteenth century, contains a number of memorials to the Filmer family. If the church is open, note in particular the unusually long brass on the floor of the north chapel, and a stained glass window showing in full dress uniform, the last baronet, killed in the First World War.

In the sixteenth century the Filmer family lived at Charlton Court (59) (grid reference 835493) on the lower slopes of a valley to the east of East Sutton. Its elaborate shaped gables were built by successors to the Filmers round the original house.

On the other side of this valley (grid reference 837495) you will see hoppers' huts, originally set up to house temporary hop pickers, many of whom came from the East End for the hop picking season. Hops are still grown in the fields to the north.

Ulcombe Church

According to legend, William the Conqueror himself stood on the site of the ragstone church at Ulcombe (60) (grid reference 847497), the valley of the owl, and gave orders for its building. Certainly of Norman origin, as you can see from the outlines from two Norman windows in the north wall of the Nave, the Church of All Saints acquired many later additions, with a fourteenth-century chancel, an Early English sanctuary and a Decorated lady chapel. Ulcombe church was one of those on the old pilgrim route along the ridge, leading to Canterbury.

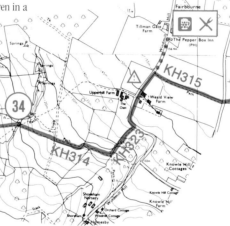

The church is unusually large for its setting, as a College of Priests was established there by Archbishop Stephen Langton between 1213 and 1215. Look for the five carved misericords which are assumed to be those of the five priests of the college. Look also for the fine brasses in the north chapel of some of the St Leger family and for the medieval wall paintings especially those in the south aisle. One shows Dives and Lazarus, the other shows the devil and St Michael weighing souls.

Some claim that the yew tree near the entrance is at least one thousand years

old. Recent research suggests it may be much older still.

In the area round Liverton Street (grid reference 874500), you will find stretches of coppiced woodland, a feature familiar throughout Kent. As the oak woodlands were cut down to provide timber for building, charcoal and other purposes, thick undergrowth grew up, often with hazel, as here. The trees were cut off at the stumps to produce a growth of young branches for periodic cutting.

The Greensand Way to the east of Ulcombe takes you into a small combe with an unusual number of springs. Be sure here to keep to the track. Even in a drought period the ground can be very wet underfoot.

INTERESTING FEATURES

50 Ladds Court
This house displays contrasting use of materials ranging from medieval half-timbering to Georgian red brick and ragstone garden walls.

51 St Michael's Church, Chart Sutton
Locally quarried ragstone was used in the 14th century to build the tower, in 1779-82 the nave and in 1897 the chancel.

52 St Mary's Church, Sutton Valence
The original 14th-century church was rebuilt in 1823-8 in local ragstone. The octagonal font is Perpendicular in style.

53 Roman Road
The probable alignment of a Roman road which ran between Rochester (Dvrobrivae) and Lympne (Portvs Lemanis).

54 Sutton Valence School
William Lambe, a clothworker, originally founded this public school in 1578. A complete set of new buildings came in 1910-14.

55 Sutton Valence Castle
The ruins of a 12th-century ragstone keep built to monitor the important medieval route across the Weald from Rye in East Sussex to Maidstone.

56 East Sutton Park
Dating from 1570 this rambling red-brick mansion was added to at various times by successive generations of the Filmers.

57 Church of St Peter and St Paul, East Sutton
Essentially the church belongs to the 14th century, with remodelling in the following two centuries. There are monuments to members of the Filmer family.

58 Prison
During the Civil Wars the modern prison, then a private house, was the setting for a battle between Sir Robert Filmer of East Sutton Park, a supporter of the King, and General Fairfax of the Parliamentarians.

59 Charlton Court.
Sir Robert Filmer, on buying East Sutton Park, kept Charlton Count, which he already owned, for a few years. An interesting fragment of the original house, belonging to him, dated 1612, can be seen in the east gable.

60 All Saint's Church, Ulcombe
Once a collegiate church, this handsome ragstone building has a complex history. The interior has been restored with sensitivity and contains interesting features.

Orange tip butterfly

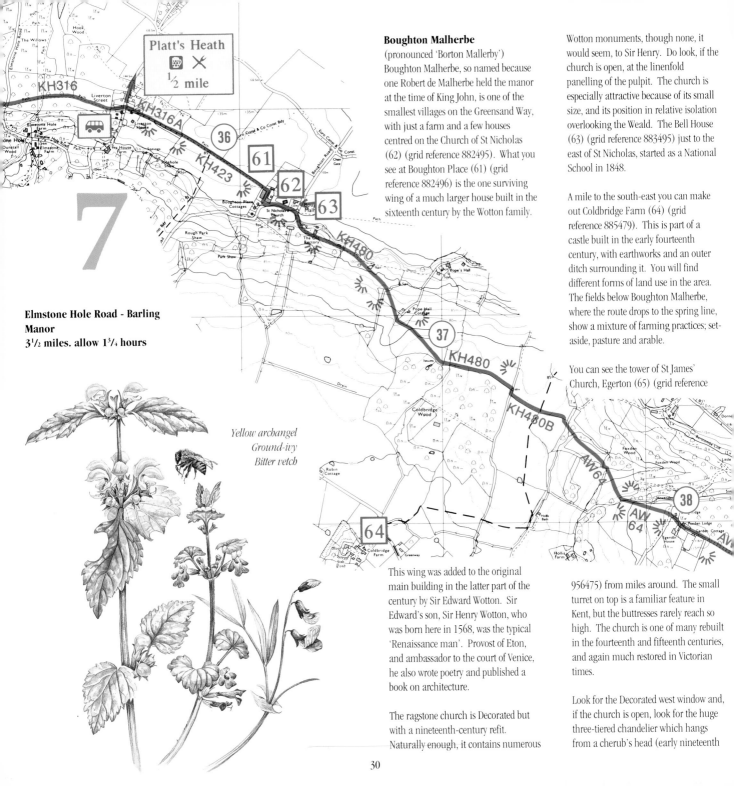

Platt's Heath
1/2 mile

KH316

KH316A

36

KH423

61

62

63

7

Elmstone Hole Road - Barling Manor
3½ miles. allow 1¾ hours

Yellow archangel
Ground-ivy
Bitter vetch

Boughton Malherbe

(pronounced 'Borton Mallerby')
Boughton Malherbe, so named because one Robert de Malherbe held the manor at the time of King John, is one of the smallest villages on the Greensand Way, with just a farm and a few houses centred on the Church of St Nicholas (62) (grid reference 882495). What you see at Boughton Place (61) (grid reference 882496) is the one surviving wing of a much larger house built in the sixteenth century by the Wotton family.

This wing was added to the original main building in the latter part of the century by Sir Edward Wotton. Sir Edward's son, Sir Henry Wotton, who was born here in 1568, was the typical 'Renaissance man'. Provost of Eton, and ambassador to the court of Venice, he also wrote poetry and published a book on architecture.

The ragstone church is Decorated but with a nineteenth-century refit. Naturally enough, it contains numerous

Wotton monuments, though none, it would seem, to Sir Henry. Do look, if the church is open, at the linenfold panelling of the pulpit. The church is especially attractive because of its small size, and its position in relative isolation overlooking the Weald. The Bell House (63) (grid reference 883495) just to the east of St Nicholas, started as a National School in 1848.

A mile to the south-east you can make out Coldbridge Farm (64) (grid reference 885479). This is part of a castle built in the early fourteenth century, with earthworks and an outer ditch surrounding it. You will find different forms of land use in the area. The fields below Boughton Malherbe, where the route drops to the spring line, show a mixture of farming practices; set-aside, pasture and arable.

You can see the tower of St James' Church, Egerton (65) (grid reference 956475) from miles around. The small turret on top is a familiar feature in Kent, but the buttresses rarely reach so high. The church is one of many rebuilt in the fourteenth and fifteenth centuries, and again much restored in Victorian times.

Look for the Decorated west window and, if the church is open, look for the huge three-tiered chandelier which hangs from a cherub's head (early nineteenth

KH480

37

KH480

KH480B

AW64

38

AW64

64

Egerton Church

The ragstone building has an ornate bell-gable.

century). The altar rail, showing St Thomas Becket, St Augustine and other saints kneeling to support it, was made in 1958.

INTERESTING FEATURES

61 Boughton Place
Dating from 1530, the house was the house of the Wotton family, notably the Elizabethan diplomat and poet, Sir Henry Wotton.

62 St Nicholas' Church, Boughton Malherbe
A small medieval ragstone church of which the chancel was rebuilt in 1848-50 and containing several Wotton monuments.

63 Bell House
Adjacent to the church is a house built as a National School in 1848.

64 Coldbridge Farm
The stone farmhouse standing within an earthwork and outer ditch forms part of a castle built by Fulk de Peyforer after 1314.

65 St James' Church, Egerton
The ragstone church was rebuilt in the 14th century, and the magnificent tower added in the 15th century. Restoration work was undertaken in Victorian times.

EGERTON

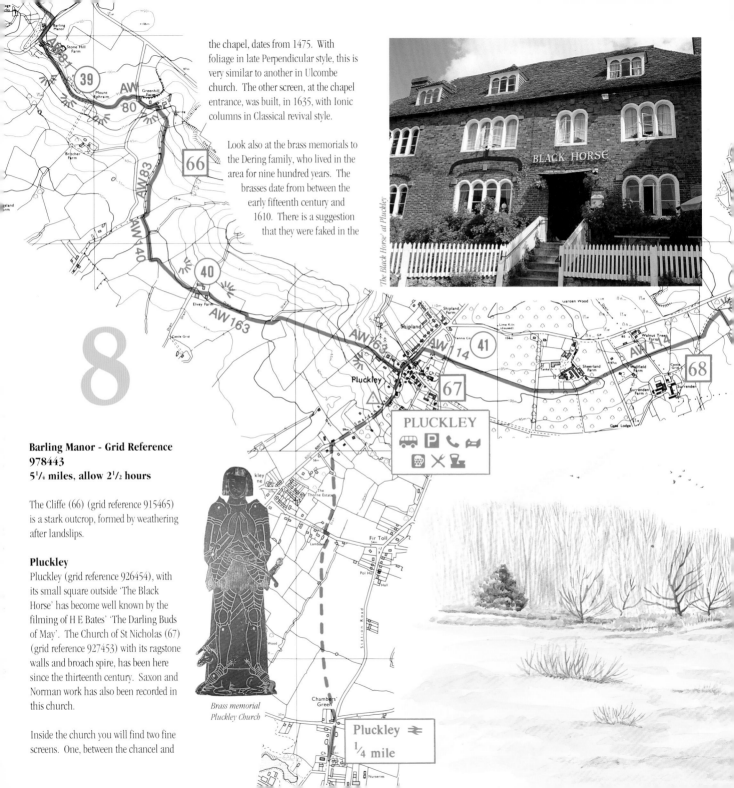

the chapel, dates from 1475. With foliage in late Perpendicular style, this is very similar to another in Ulcombe church. The other screen, at the chapel entrance, was built, in 1635, with Ionic columns in Classical revival style.

Look also at the brass memorials to the Dering family, who lived in the area for nine hundred years. The brasses date from between the early fifteenth century and 1610. There is a suggestion that they were faked in the

'The Black Horse' at Pluckley

Barling Manor - Grid Reference 978443
5¼ miles, allow 2½ hours

The Cliffe (66) (grid reference 915465) is a stark outcrop, formed by weathering after landslips.

Pluckley

Pluckley (grid reference 926454), with its small square outside 'The Black Horse' has become well known by the filming of H E Bates' 'The Darling Buds of May'. The Church of St Nicholas (67) (grid reference 927453) with its ragstone walls and broach spire, has been here since the thirteenth century. Saxon and Norman work has also been recorded in this church.

Inside the church you will find two fine screens. One, between the chancel and

Brass memorial Pluckley Church

PLUCKLEY

Pluckley ⇥ ¼ mile

With its claim to twelve ghosts Pluckley ranks high among the country's most haunted villages. It certainly has no rival in Kent. The ghosts include a phantom coach and horses, a highwayman who died in a fight and a Red Lady who grieves in the churchyard.

A descendant of Sir Edward Dering, Sir Edward Cholmely Dering, had the local houses built in identical style, all with arched windows. He thought the design would bring good luck. According to tradition, the sixteenth-century Sir Edward, fleeing from the Parlimentarians, jumped to safety through one such window in the Civil Wars.

The same Sir Edward also built Surrenden or Surrenden Dering (68) (grid reference 939454) lost in a fire in 1952. The stables are similar to those at seventeenth century by Sir Edward Dering, to enhance his family reputation. The costume and armour look authentic enough.

Hothfield Common

Bell heather

A20 Charing 2½ miles

A20 Ashford 3 miles

LITTLE CHART

HOTHFIELD

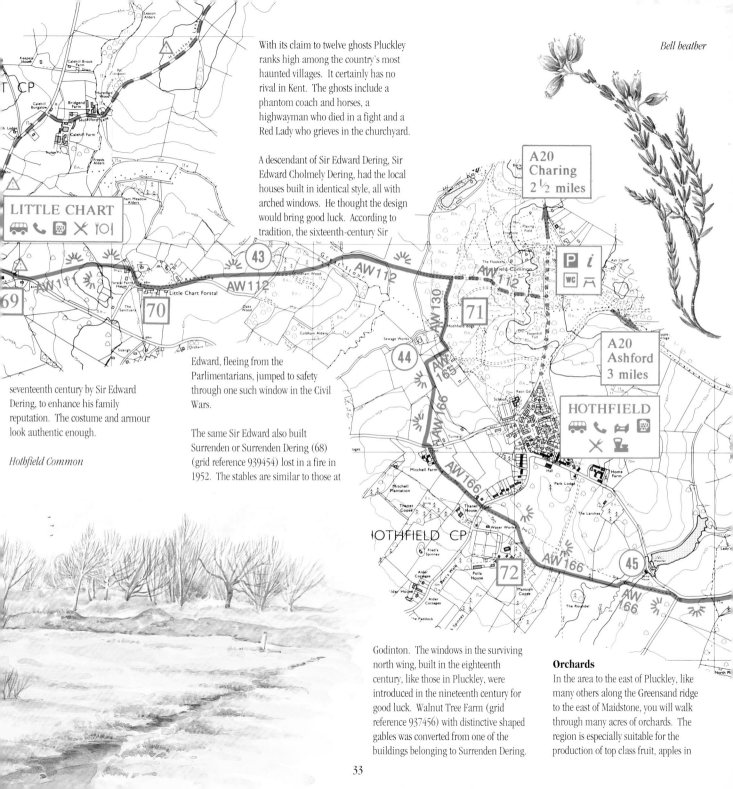

Godinton. The windows in the surviving north wing, built in the eighteenth century, like those in Pluckley, were introduced in the nineteenth century for good luck. Walnut Tree Farm (grid reference 937456) with distinctive shaped gables was converted from one of the buildings belonging to Surrenden Dering.

Orchards

In the area to the east of Pluckley, like many others along the Greensand ridge to the east of Maidstone, you will walk through many acres of orchards. The region is especially suitable for the production of top class fruit, apples in particular. The soil is well drained and the land is freer from late spring frosts which settle in the valleys and can destroy a crop overnight.

Apples were first introduced to Kent from continental Europe, first by the Romans and later by the Dutch and French from the fifteenth century. Acreage has reduced this century but modern research, as well as demand, ensures that they remain an important aspect of Kent horticulture and scenery. You will see a number of newly planted orchards. Note the smaller species now growing to facilitate picking.

Little Chart

Little Chart (grid reference 943459) lies in a small valley where the Great Stour opens into old mill ponds. The Church of St Mary (69) (grid reference 944458) was built in 1955 to replace the medieval church which was bombed in the Second World War and considered too damaged for repair. The ruins of the old church, which include a Perpendicular west tower, stand two-thirds of a mile to the north-west. In the village you will find more of the Dering windows and more Dutch gables.

From the rise to either side of Little Chart you can see the Pilgrims' Way running below the tree line on the North Downs. This is an ancient trackway used from early times both because it avoided the dense woods of the Weald below and because it provided water along the spring line. It later became the pilgrim route to Canterbury.

The Great Stour flows eastwards to Ashford, then northwards through Canterbury, reaching the sea at

Sandwich. Little Chart Forstal (grid reference 955459) is set round a Green on higher ground above the Stour Valley. The name Forstal, found frequently in place names in Kent, means land in front of a farm building. From 1931 until his death in 1974, H E Bates lived at The Granary (70) (grid reference 952458), which he and his wife had converted from an old barn.

View of the Weald near Pluckley

Hothfield Common

Hothfield Common (71) (grid reference 970460) is a National Nature Reserve, maintained by the Kent Trust for Nature Conservation (KTNC). The Common lies on a sandy plateau with impermeable clay below. The clay forces water to resurface as acid springs. The resulting water-logged conditions have led to the slow build-up of peat bogs where you will find numerous mosses, bog asphodel and marsh St John's wort. Both the bogland, which forms part of the area, and the heathland beside the bog are rare habitats in Kent and contain unusual and important insects as well as plants and breeding birds.

Heathland and lowland bogs come about with the clearance of woodland and the introduction of livestock grazing in sandy areas with nutrient poor soil or peat. They were fashioned over centuries and in many instances, over several millennia. Such sites support rare communities of highly specialised plants and animals. Hothfield Common is a very ancient site, the last remaining heath and bog complex left in Kent. Grazing ceased at the turn of the century with the collapse of rural agricultural economies.

In 1992 KTNC began a restoration programme of bracken and birch

clearance and re-introduced effective livestock grazing for the first time this century. Gradually areas of heather heath and purple moor grass will replace invasive bracken and birch. In the woodland are birch, sycamore, oak, hawthorn and sweet chestnut. Birds include woodpeckers, treecreepers and the tree pipit.

The Greensand Way takes you to the west of the main bog along a concrete causeway, really the line of a sewage pipe which has served as a dam. Under no circumstances should you explore the bogs themselves. Use the bridge or causeway, as the bogs, especially the main bog, are deep.

Hothfield Common

St Margaret's Church, Hothfield

The tower of St Margaret's Church in Hothfield (72) (grid reference 969445) is Decorated with a needle spire rising from its tower. It is shingled, that is, clad in heavy wooden 'tiles'.

If you can get in, look for the monument to Sir John Tufton who died in 1624. He rebuilt the church, some years after lightning had struck down the original in 1598. This explains the late Perpendicular windows, giving much more light than those of an earlier date. It also explains why Sir John merited such a magnificent monument, including a sea-lion at his own feet, a lion's paw at his wife's.

In Hothfield churchyard beside a yew tree next to the path is a headstone to one Sarah Stanford who died of smallpox in 1790. On it is the epitaph:

Her soul without a spot is gone to heaven;
Her spotted body to the worms is given.'

The lengths of huge and buttressed old walling you see beside the roads in Hothfield survive from the old Hothfield Place, designed by James Wyatt for the Earl of Thanet, but pulled down in 1954. The parkland to the east of the church crossed by the Greensand Way also formed part of this estate.

INTERESTING FEATURES

66 The Cliffe

The cliffs here and beside the route immediately south of Egerton are outcrops formed by weathering after landslips.

67 Church of St Nicholas, Pluckley

The mainly 13th-century church contains a collection of 15th to 17th-century brasses to the local Dering family.

68 Surrenden Dering

Sir Edward Dering's red-brick house of 1632 was burnt down in 1952. The north wing is of the 18th century, whilst its windows were inserted a century later.

69 St Mary's Church, Little Chart

A neo-Gothic Church built in 1955 to replace the medieval one two-thirds of a mile away destroyed by Second World War bombing.

70 The Granary

H E Bates, the author, lived here from 1931 until his death in 1974. He and his wife had converted it from an old barn.

71 Hothfield Common Nature Reserve

Once part of the Manor of Hothfield, the area was never cultivated, but had commoners' rights. The Common with its bogs and heathland was designated an SSSI in 1985.

72 St Margaret's Church, Hothfield

This medieval church with its short shingled spire was largely rebuilt in the 17th century, as the nave had been destroyed by lightning.

9

'Hooden Horse' at Great Chart

**Grid Reference 978443 -
Chilmington Quarry
3 miles, allow 1½ hours**

Godinton

The route skirts Godinton Park (grid reference 984438), parkland which contains many old oaks. One, known as the Domesday oak, fell on 3 September 1939 at the moment of Chamberlain's broadcast announcing the declaration of war with Germany.

At the centre of the park is Godinton House (73) (grid reference 982439) which is well worth a visit in season. Captain Nicholas Toke rebuilt its east front in brick with shaped gables and mullioned windows in 1628.

Great Chart

Great Chart used to be much larger than at present, with a second main street. Today it shows little sign that once it was more important than Ashford, which replaced it as the river crossing.

Most of Great Chart lies on the one street, where you will see the shaped gables on the almshouses (75) (grid reference 982420) built in 1833, and the school, built in 1835. The Tokes of Godinton, Lords of this manor too, were responsible for these. The Church of St Mary the Virgin (76) (grid reference 980419) stands on higher ground at the top of the main street.

The church contains some fine memorials, tablets and brasses. The Toke family owned the north chapel and you will find memorials to various of their number. Nicholas Toke, who died in 1680, is remembered in a brass on the floor, with five wives and three daughters. Tradition has it that there might have been a sixth wife had he not died while walking to London to seek her. He was 93 at the time. The building at the gate is known as the Pest House (77) (grid reference 979419), assuming it was used to isolate people with infectious diseases. A meeting place is a more likely explanation.

Godinton Park

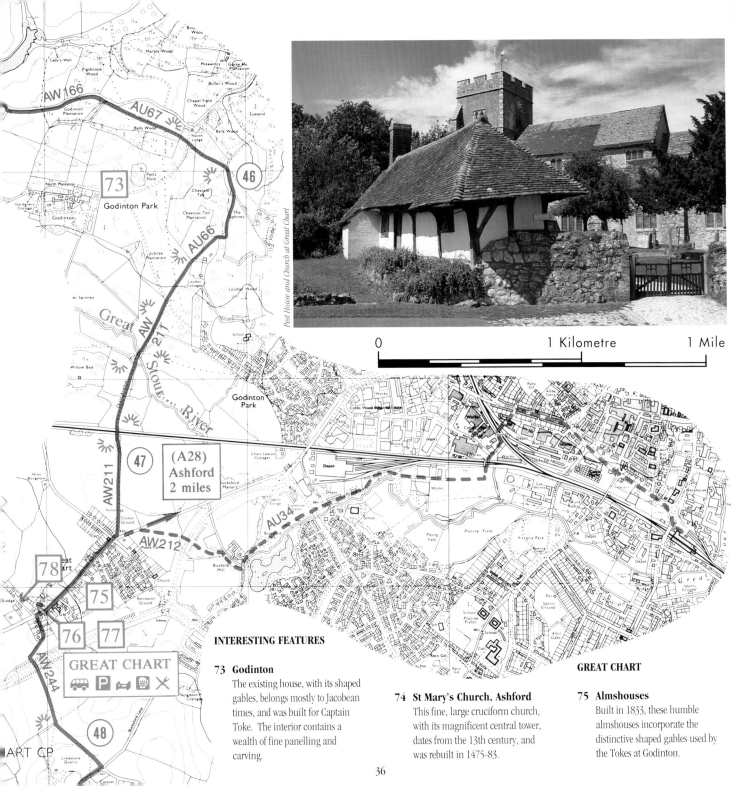

Pest House and Church at Great Chart

0   1 Kilometre   1 Mile

INTERESTING FEATURES

73 Godinton

The existing house, with its shaped gables, belongs mostly to Jacobean times, and was built for Captain Toke. The interior contains a wealth of fine panelling and carving.

74 St Mary's Church, Ashford

This fine, large cruciform church, with its magnificent central tower, dates from the 13th century, and was rebuilt in 1475-83.

GREAT CHART

75 Almshouses

Built in 1833, these humble almshouses incorporate the distinctive shaped gables used by the Tokes at Godinton.

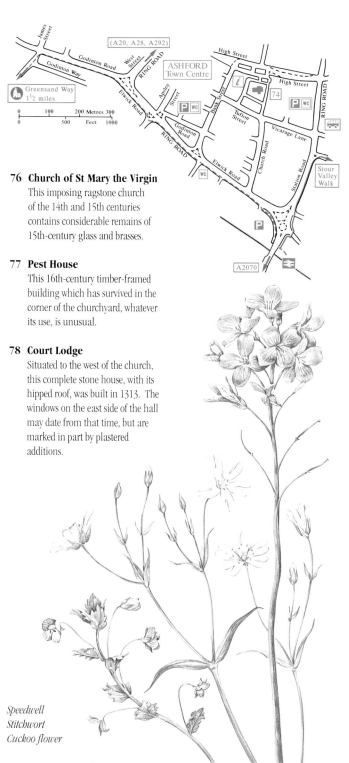

76 Church of St Mary the Virgin

This imposing ragstone church of the 14th and 15th centuries contains considerable remains of 15th-century glass and brasses.

77 Pest House

This 16th-century timber-framed building which has survived in the corner of the churchyard, whatever its use, is unusual.

78 Court Lodge

Situated to the west of the church, this complete stone house, with its hipped roof, was built in 1313. The windows on the east side of the hall may date from that time, but are marked in part by plastered additions.

Speedwell
Stitchwort
Cuckoo flower

Chilmington Quarry - Hamstreet Railway Station
7 miles, allow 3½ hours

From the top of the hill by the limestone quarry (78) (grid reference 982412), now infilled, you can see the flood plain of the Great Stour to the north. Once, this was a wide estuary until alluvium silted it up to give the present fertile land. On the North Downs beyond you can again see clearly the route of the Pilgrims' Way running below the tree line.

Romney Marsh

At the top of Mock Lane (grid reference 980409) you are standing on the old cliff-line which curves round from Cliff End to Hythe. Below, to the south, stretches Romney Marsh, once a huge bay. The cliff-line was still very clear in Anglo-Saxon times but silting had begun long before. Marshland developed first because of upward movement of the sea bed, then from deposits of alluvium from rivers such as the Rother. Now, fully drained, the Romney Marsh forms an area used largely for sheep grazing and wheat production.

Kingsnorth (grid reference 002394) stretches along the slope of a rise facing north towards Ashford. On the top is the late fourteenth-century Church of St Michael and All Angels (81) (grid reference 006392). It is small, with few decorations, but has attractive stained glass windows from the fifteenth century. Look especially for the window showing St Michael himself. Diminutive weather-boarded Mouse Hall (80) beside the church gate was built in the fifteenth century.

A battery of 'Super Heavy' railway guns was located in Golden Wood during the Second World War, for defence against a possible German invasion. From the Greensand Way you can still see the huts in Golden Wood which housed the gun crews (82) (grid reference 012366). A spur was led off the Ashford-Rye railway line to accommodate the wagons on which the guns, their ammunition and their stores were installed and transported.

Ham Street Woods

Ham Street Woods (grid reference 006338), lying on the southern edge of

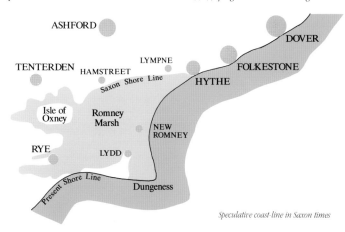

Speculative coast-line in Saxon times

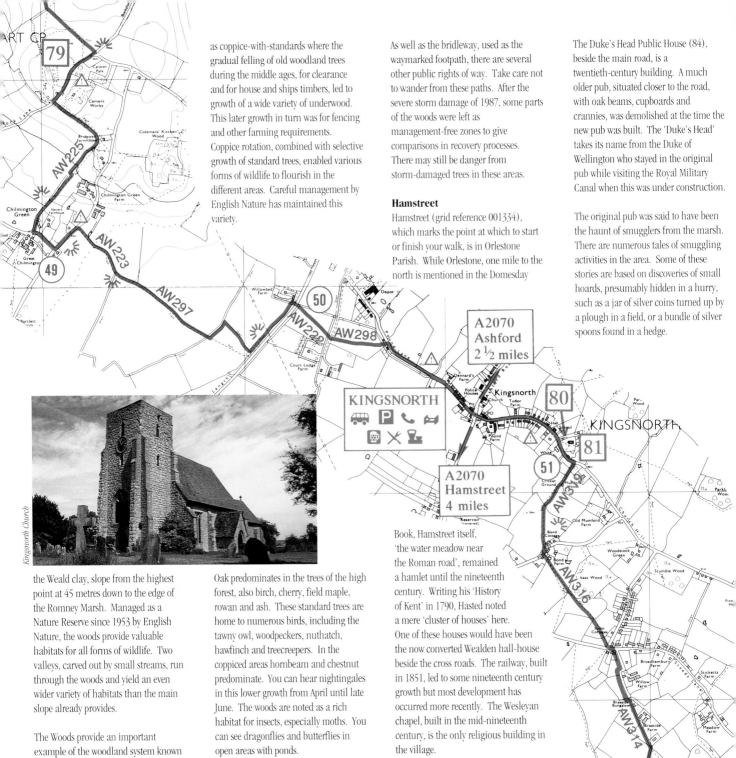

as coppice-with-standards where the gradual felling of old woodland trees during the middle ages, for clearance and for house and ships timbers, led to growth of a wide variety of underwood. This later growth in turn was for fencing and other farming requirements. Coppice rotation, combined with selective growth of standard trees, enabled various forms of wildlife to flourish in the different areas. Careful management by English Nature has maintained this variety.

As well as the bridleway, used as the waymarked footpath, there are several other public rights of way. Take care not to wander from these paths. After the severe storm damage of 1987, some parts of the woods were left as management-free zones to give comparisons in recovery processes. There may still be danger from storm-damaged trees in these areas.

Hamstreet

Hamstreet (grid reference 001334), which marks the point at which to start or finish your walk, is in Orlestone Parish. While Orlestone, one mile to the north is mentioned in the Domesday

The Duke's Head Public House (84), beside the main road, is a twentieth-century building. A much older pub, situated closer to the road, with oak beams, cupboards and crannies, was demolished at the time the new pub was built. The 'Duke's Head' takes its name from the Duke of Wellington who stayed in the original pub while visiting the Royal Military Canal when this was under construction.

The original pub was said to have been the haunt of smugglers from the marsh. There are numerous tales of smuggling activities in the area. Some of these stories are based on discoveries of small hoards, presumably hidden in a hurry, such as a jar of silver coins turned up by a plough in a field, or a bundle of silver spoons found in a hedge.

Kingsnorth Church

the Weald clay, slope from the highest point at 45 metres down to the edge of the Romney Marsh. Managed as a Nature Reserve since 1953 by English Nature, the woods provide valuable habitats for all forms of wildlife. Two valleys, carved out by small streams, run through the woods and yield an even wider variety of habitats than the main slope already provides.

The Woods provide an important example of the woodland system known

Oak predominates in the trees of the high forest, also birch, cherry, field maple, rowan and ash. These standard trees are home to numerous birds, including the tawny owl, woodpeckers, nuthatch, hawfinch and treecreepers. In the coppiced areas hornbeam and chestnut predominate. You can hear nightingales in this lower growth from April until late June. The woods are noted as a rich habitat for insects, especially moths. You can see dragonflies and butterflies in open areas with ponds.

Book, Hamstreet itself, 'the water meadow near the Roman road', remained a hamlet until the nineteenth century. Writing his 'History of Kent' in 1790, Hasted noted a mere 'cluster of houses' here. One of these houses would have been the now converted Wealden hall-house beside the cross roads. The railway, built in 1851, led to some nineteenth century growth but most development has occurred more recently. The Wesleyan chapel, built in the mid-nineteenth century, is the only religious building in the village.

Royal Military Canal

To the south at Ham Street Bridge (grid reference 004324) on the A2070, you will find the Royal Military Canal (85) which runs across Romney Marsh from Hythe to Rye. This was built between 1804 and 1809 to help to defend the rest of England from the much-feared invasion by Napoleon. As a bonus, it was also intended to have practical value in catching water from the higher ground and so relieving flood water on the marsh, as well as providing a means of transport for shingle from the beaches for road making.

There was even a scheme to link the canal with a vast network of canals throughout Kent and open up the interior of Kent to give access to the sea via Canterbury, Chatham, Rye and Hythe. The canal's ability to protect the country from invasion was never put to the test. During the nineteenth century it provided a useful means of transport. The National Rivers Authority now controls most of the canal, with Shepway Borough Council controlling the Hythe section.

The overall line of the canal is north-east/south-west, but as you stand at Ham Street Bridge you will find it does not run in a straight line. A bend in the alignment occurs every third of a mile throughout the canal's entire length. It was so built that gun positions would be provided at the end of each length to flank the crossings.

Royal Mail Stamps

As you study the Ordnance Survey map of the Hamstreet area you may recall the Royal Mail stamps of September 1991, issued to mark the bicentenary of Ordnance Survey as the official mapping agency for Great Britain. These show the village of Hamstreet as depicted in Ordnance Survey maps published during the last two centuries. They show the

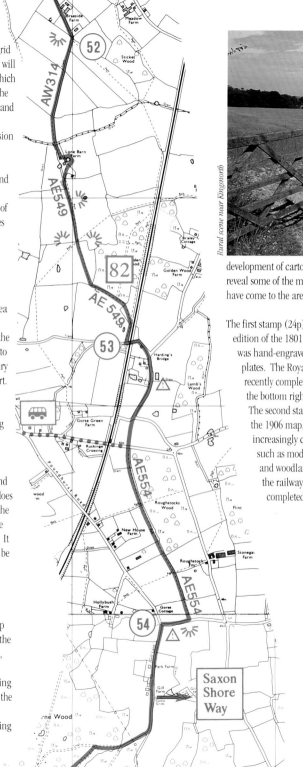

Rural scene near Kingsnorth

development of cartography and also reveal some of the major changes that have come to the area.

The first stamp (24p) shows the 1816 edition of the 1801 map of Kent, which was hand-engraved on copper plates. The Royal Military Canal, recently completed, appears in the bottom right-hand corner. The second stamp (28p) shows the 1906 map, with increasingly complex symbols, such as modern contour lines and woodlands. It also gives the railway which had been completed in 1851. The third

stamp (33p) shows the 1959 map, now bearing symbols for electricity lines. Now, too, you can see the chapel and post office. The fourth stamp (39p) shows the 1991 edition of the Ordnance Survey map. This time you find additional details such as the new symbol for orchards, and the change in road colouring; red for A roads, brown for B roads, etc. The Saxon Shore Way long-distance path appears on this map for the first time.

The stamps summarise the importance of the Ordnance Survey not only as guides to the countryside but as a record of social and economic development.

Saxon Shore

For a short distance the Greensand Way coincides with part of the Saxon Shore Way, a long-distance route which traces the old shore line from Gravesend on the Thames estuary to Rye on the Kent-Sussex border. The name 'Saxon Shore' comes from a series of fortifications built by the Romans, mainly in the late fourth century, to defend the country against raids by Saxon pirates in the English Channel and the North Sea areas.

Situated at the mouths of the main rivers, these forts contained troops and a fleet to give chase to the marauders and provided a frontier between the civilised and the barbarian world. The Saxon Shore Way passes four of these old forts along the way, Reculver, Richborough, Dover and Lympne, as well as many other places of historic interest, including Rochester and Sandwich. While the coastline has receded in several places, you find estuary and sea views for much of the way. Between Hythe and Rye the route follows the high ground of the ancient cliff. The entire footpath runs for 140 miles.

INTERESTING FEATURES

79 Chilmington Quarry
Now infilled, this quarry once supplied limestone for local building and agricultural use.

80 Mouse Hall
The small 15th-century weather-boarded building beside the churchgate is a private house.

81 Church of St Michael and All Angels, Kingsnorth
Within this 14th-century church is some 15th-century glass, notably a window portraying the complete figure of St Michael.

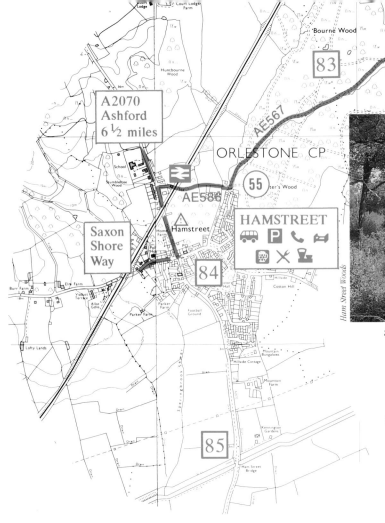

Ham Street Woods

82 Gun Emplacement
The site of a battery of super-heavy railway guns during the Second World War against a possible German invasion.

83 Ham Street Woods National Nature Reserve
Five woods covering 97 hectares comprise the Reserve, which is situated on the southern edge of the Weald where it slopes down towards Romney Marsh.

84 Duke's Head Public House
Named after the Duke of Wellington, the public house stands near the site of an older pub which was a smugglers' haunt.

85 Royal Military Canal
The Royal Military Canal was built between 1804 and 1809 primarily as a defensive feature against a possible Napoleonic invasion.

Royal Military Canal

INTERESTING PLACES TO VISIT
on or near the Greensand Way

Squerryes Court (NT)
Westerham
tel: Westerham (0959) 62345/63118

Quebec House (NT)
Westerham
tel: Westerham (0959) 62206

Chartwell (NT)
Westerham
tel: Edenbridge (0732) 866368

Riverhill House (HHA)
Sevenoaks
tel: Sevenoaks (0732) 452557/458802

Knole (NT)
Sevenoaks
tel: Sevenoaks (0732) 450608

Sevenoaks Museum and Art Gallery
Buckhurst Lane, Sevenoaks
tel: Sevenoaks (0732) 453118

Ightham Mote (NT)
Ivy Hatch, Sevenoaks
tel: Plaxtol (0732) 810378

Old Soar Manor (NT/EH)
Plaxtol, Borough Green
tel: Medway (0634) 832666

Boughton Monchelsea Place (HHA)
Boughton Monchelsea, Maidstone
tel: Maidstone (0622) 743120

Sutton Valence Castle (EH)
Sutton Valence, Maidstone
tel: Medway (0634) 832666

Godinton House (HHA)
Ashford
tel: Ashford (0233) 620773

Parish Churches

(keys usually obtained locally if not open)

Key:
NT   National Trust
EH   English Heritage
HHA Historic Houses Association

COUNTRYSIDE OPEN SPACES
on or near the Greensand Way

Limpsfield Chart

Crockhamhill Common

Toys Hill
National Trust
tel: Lamberhurst (0892) 890651

Ide Hill
National Trust
tel: Lamberhurst (0892) 890651

Bough Beech Reservoir
(by permit only)
Kent Trust for Nature Conservation
tel: Maidstone (0622) 753017/759017

Emmetts Garden
National Trust
tel: Ide Hill (073 275) 367/429

Hanging Bank & Brockhoult Mount
Kent County Council
tel: Maidstone (0622) 696411

Knole Park
(open to pedestrians by courtesy of Lord Sackville)

One Tree Hill
National Trust
tel: Lamberhurst (0892) 890651

Shipbourne Common

Dene Park, Shipbourne
(1 mile south south-west of Dunk's Green)

Yalding Lees

Hothfield Common
Kent Trust for Nature Conservation
tel: Maidstone (0622) 753017/759017

Hamstreet Woods
English Nature
tel: Wye (0233) 812525

For further information and details about most of these open spaces please see the leaflet 'Out and About in the Kent Countryside' available from the Planning Department, Kent County Council, Springfield, Maidstone, Kent ME14 2LX, telephone Maidstone (0622) 696411.

OTHER WALKING OPPORTUNITIES

If you have enjoyed this walk and would like to explore other waymarked walking routes in Kent, write to the Access and Recreation Officer (listed elsewhere) for a publications price list. In series with the 'Greensand Way' are the 'Stour Valley Walk' and 'Eden Valley Walk'. Other route guidebooks are planned and in preparation.

It is possible for you to devise your own shorter linear and circular walks using the extensive rights of way network throughout the county. Information about these can be obtained by studying either the Ordnance Survey Pathfinder maps or the Kent County Council Definitive Maps of Public Rights of Way. Copies of the latter can be inspected at public libraries or district council offices. In the event of difficulty please contact the Public Rights of Way Manager (listed elsewhere).

Linked to the Greensand Way in Kent are a number of other linear walks, as follows:

Vanguard Way
The Vanguard Way is a 63 mile route from the London suburbs at Croydon to the English Channel at Seaford. It crosses the North and South Downs and the Kent, Surrey and Sussex Weald. The route crosses the Greensand Way at Limpsfield Chart.

Publications:
'The Vanguard Way' - Vanguard Rambling Club, c/o 109 Selsdon Park Road, South Croydon, Surrey CR2 8JJ.

'The Wealdway and the Vanguard Way' - Kev Reynolds, Cicerone Press, 2 Police Square, Milnthorpe, Cumbria.

London Countryway
The route of the London Countryway is a complete 205 mile circuit around London and keeps between 13 and 31 miles from the centre of the capital. The route coincides with the Greensand Way between Goodley Stock and Ightham Mote.

Publication:
'A Guide to the London Countryway' - Keith Chesterton, Constable and Co, 10 Orange Street, London WC2H 7EG.

Wealdway
Following an 80 mile route from the Thames Estuary at Gravesend to the English Channel at Beachy Head, the Wealdway crosses the North and South Downs and the Kent and Sussex Weald. The route coincides with a short section of the Greensand Way at West Peckham.

Publications:
'Wealdway' - Geoffrey King, Wealdway Group, c/o 11 Old London Road, Brighton, East Sussex BN1 8XR
'Wealdway Accommodation Guide' - Wealdway Group as above.
'Guide to the Wealdway' - John H Mason, Constable and Co, 11 Orange Street, London WC2H 3EW

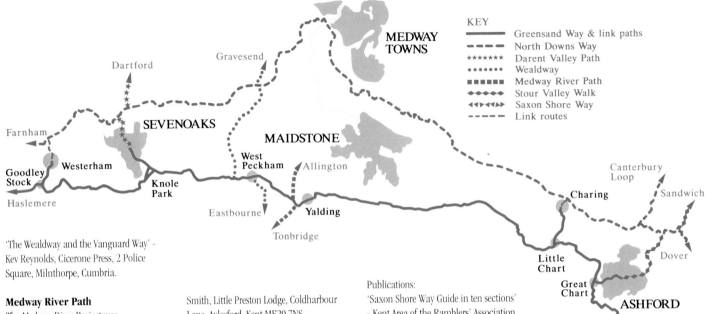

KEY

— Greensand Way & link paths
- - - North Downs Way
★★★★★★★ Darent Valley Path
••••••• Wealdway
▬▬▬▬▬▬ Medway River Path
◆◆◆◆◆◆ Stour Valley Walk
◄▶◄▶◄▶ Saxon Shore Way
- - - Link routes

MEDWAY TOWNS

Dartford
Gravesend
SEVENOAKS
MAIDSTONE
Farnham
Westerham
Knole Park
West Peckham
Allington
Canterbury Loop
Charing
Sandwich
Goodley Stock
Haslemere
Eastbourne
Yalding
Tonbridge
Little Chart
Great Chart
Dover
ASHFORD
Gravesend
Rye
Hamstreet

'The Wealdway and the Vanguard Way' - Kev Reynolds, Cicerone Press, 2 Police Square, Milnthorpe, Cumbria.

Medway River Path

The Medway River Project was established in 1988 to enhance public access, amenity and nature conservation along the River Medway. The project promotes local community action in caring for the countryside. The planned continuous riverside path is open at present between Tonbridge and Yalding and between Wateringbury and Allington.

Publications:
'River Valley Walks in Kent - River Medway' - Medway RiverProject, 3 Lock Cottages, Lock Lane, Sandling, Maidstone, Kent ME17 3AL and Kent County Council Planning Department, Springfield, Maidstone, Kent ME14 2LX.

Maidstone Circular Walk

This walk, which provides a circular walk around Maidstone, utilises part of the Greensand Way and provides a link with the North Downs Way.

Publication:
'Maidstone Circular Walk' - Ramblers' Association (Maidstone Group), Mr A

Smith, Little Preston Lodge, Coldharbour Lane, Aylesford, Kent ME20 7NS

Stour Valley Walk

Running for 38 miles between Ashford and Sandwich, the Stour Valley Walk passes through a gap in the North Downs, visits the historic city of Canterbury, and follows the ancient Saxon Shore line to the south of the former Wantsum Sea Channel. Access to the route is via a link path from the Greensand Way at Great Chart.

Publication:
'Stour Valley Walk' - Kent County Council, Planning Department, Springfield, Maidstone, Kent ME14 2LX.

Saxon Shore Way

The south-eastern end of the Greensand Way links with the Saxon Shore Way, a 140 mile route which traces the old shore line from Gravesend on the Thames Estuary to Rye in East Sussex. The name comes from a series of fortifications built by the Romans to defend the country against Saxon pirate raids.

Publications:
'Saxon Shore Way Guide in ten sections' - Kent Area of the Ramblers' Association, c/o Mr P Miller, 104 Hamelin Road, Darland, Gillingham, Kent ME7 3ER

FURTHER READING

Building of England (The)
West Kent and the Weald
John Newman
Penguin

Classic Landforms of the Weald
D A Robinson and R B G Williams
The Geographical Association

Companion Guide to Kent and Sussex (The)
Keith Spence
Collins

Continuity and Colonisation
A Everitt
Leicester University Press

County Sites and Monument Record
Planning Department
Kent County Council

Hopping Down in Kent
Alan Bignell
Robert Hale Ltd

Hops and Hop Picking
Richard Filmer
Shire publications Ltd

Kent - A Shell Guide
Pennethorne Hughes
Faber and Faber

Place Names of Kent (The)
Judith Glover
Batsford

Place Names of Kent (The)
J K Wallenberg
Upsala

Roman Britain
Historical Map and Guide
Ordnance Survey

Roman Ways in the Weald
Ivan Margary
Phoenix House

Weald (The)
Wes Gibbons
Unwin

Weald (The)
S W Wooldridge and Frederick Goldring
Collins

Weald of Kent and Sussex
S Kaye-Smith
Robert Hale Ltd

Who's Buried Where in Kent
Alan Major
Meresborough Books

Guidebooks to the houses and churches passed en route.

GLOSSARY

Medieval Parish Church

A   Nave
1   aisle
2   nave arcade
3   clerestory
4   pier
5   arch
6   roof truss
7   pulpit
8   lectern
9   font
10   chancel arch
11   rood screen
12   doom painting

B   Chancel
13   east window
14   reredos
15   altar
16   sanctuary
17   altar rail
18   sedilia
19   piscina

C   Tower
20   turret
21   battlemented parapet
22   gargoyle
23   buttress
24   west door
25   belfry
26   ringing chamber

D   Porch
27   mass dial

E   Lych-gate

Belfry
The upper room in a tower in which bells are hung.

Bell-gable (bell-cot)
A small structure on the top of a gable in which bells are hung.

Brass
An effigy engraved on a brass plate.

Broach (spire)
The half-pyramid of stone which effects the change from a square tower to an octagonal spire.

Corinthian
The most ornate of the Greek columns having a bell-shaped capital with rows of acanthus leaves.

Cornice
A projecting decorative moulding along the top of a wall or arch.

Crown post
A roof truss consisting of a central vertical timber supporting a crown-like splay of timbers.

Crow stepped gable
A gable with step-like projections on its sloping sides.

Cupola
A small polygonal or circular domed turret crowning a roof.

Dutch gable
A concave and convex shaped gable with a flemish influence characteristic of c1580-1680.

Galleting
The use of small stones in a mortar course for decoration and reinforcement.

Gargoyle
A water spout projecting from the parapet of a wall often carved into human or animal shape.

Hatchment
A board with painted armorial bearings.

Hipped roof
A roof with sloped instead of vertical ends.

Ionic
A Greek column, whose capital is characterised by two lateral volutes (scrolls).

Lady chapel
A chapel dedicated to the Virgin Mary, usually located eastwards of the high altar in a large church.

Linenfold
Carved or moulded panelling representing a fold or scroll of linen.

Lych-gate
Wooden gate structure with a roof at the churchyard entrance providing space for the reception of a coffin.

Misericord
A ledge on the underside of a hinged wooden seat in the choir stalls, affording support during long periods of standing.

Pediment
A triangular piece of wall which is filled in and supports a sloping roof.

Rustication

External stonework cut in massive blocks and separated from each other by deep mortar joints to give an impression of great strength, especially at the base of a building.

Solar

In a medieval building, an upper room, usually the private room of the owner.

Tuscan

A simple Roman column with plain capital.

COUNTRYSIDE ACCESS CHARTER

YOUR RIGHTS OF WAY ARE

Public footpaths - on foot only. Sometimes waymarked in yellow.
Bridleways - on foot, horseback and pedal cycle. Sometimes waymarked in blue.
Byways - (usually old roads), most 'Roads Used as Public Paths' and, of course, public roads - all traffic.
Use maps, signs and waymarks. Ordnance Survey Pathfinder and Landranger maps show most public rights of way.

ON RIGHTS OF WAY YOU CAN

Take a pram, pushchair or wheelchair if practicable.
Take a dog (on a lead or under close control).
Take a short route round an illegal obstruction or remove it sufficiently to get past.

YOU HAVE A RIGHT TO GO FOR RECREATION TO

Public parks and open spaces - on foot.
Most commons near older towns and cities - on foot and sometimes on horseback.
Private land where the owner has a formal agreement with the local authority.

IN ADDITION you can use by local or established custom or consent, but ask for advice if you are unsure.
Many areas of open country like moorland, fell and coastal areas, especially those of the National Trust, and some commons.
Some woods and forests, especially those owned by the Forestry Commission.
Country parks and picnic sites.
Most beaches.
Towpaths on canals and rivers.
Some private paths and tracks.
Consent sometimes extends to riding horses and pedal cycles.

FOR YOUR INFORMATION

County and metropolitan district councils and London boroughs maintain and record rights of way, and register commons and village greens.
Obstructions, dangerous animals, harassment and misleading signs on rights of way are illegal and you should report them to the council.
Paths across fields can be ploughed; they must normally be reinstated within two weeks.
Landowners can require you to leave land to which you have no right of access.
Motor vehicles are normally permitted only on roads, byways and some 'Roads Used as Public Paths'.
Follow any local bylaws.

AND, WHEREVER YOU GO, FOLLOW THE COUNTRY CODE

Enjoy the Countryside and respect its life and work.
Guard against all risk of fire.
Fasten all gates.
Keep your dogs under close control.
Keep to public paths across farmland.
Use gates and stiles to cross fences, hedges and walls.
Leave livestock, crops and machinery alone.
Take your litter home.
Help to keep all water clean.

Protect wildlife, plants and trees.
Take special care on country roads.
Make no unnecessary noise.

This Charter is for practical guidance in England and Wales only. Fuller advice is given in a free booklet 'Out in the Country' available from Countryside Commission Publications, Printworks Lane, Levenshulme, Manchester M19 3JP, telephone 061-224 6287.

Published with kind permission of the Countryside Commission.

TABLE OF HISTORICAL PERIODS

Mesolithic	10000 - 3500BC}	
Neolithic	3500 - 2000BC}	Prehistoric
Bronze Age	2000 - 800BC}	
Iron Age	800BC - AD43}	
Roman	43 - 410	
Anglo Saxon	410 - 1066	
Norman	1066 - 1154	
Plantagenets	1154 - 1399}	
Lancastrians	1399 - 1461}	Medieval
Yorkists	1461 - 1485}	
Tudors	1485 - 1603}	
Elizabethan	1558 - 1603}	Renaissance
Stuarts	1603 - 1714}	
Jacobean	1603 - 1649}	
Commonwealth	1649 - 1660}	
Restoration	1660 - 1702}	
Anne	1702 - 1714}	
Hanoverian	1714 - 1901	
Georgian	1714 - 1837	
Regency	1810 - 1820	
Victorian	1837 - 1901	
Edwardian	1901 - 1910	
Windsor	1910 - Present Day	

TABLE OF ARCHITECTURAL PERIODS

Romanesque	1066 - 1190	
Early English	1190 - 1280	
Decorated	1280 - 1380	
Perpendicular	1380 - 1550	Gothic
Classical	1550 - 1810	
Gothic & Classical Revivals	1810 - 1914	
Modern	1914 - Present Day	